THE
WARRIOR'S
WEAPONS

•• VOLUME TWO ••

DR. UWAKWE C. CHUKWU

DR. UWAKWE CHRISTIAN CHUKWU
Hearts of Jesus and Mary Ministries
website: www.hjamm.org
Email: ucchukwu@hjamm.org
Email: ucchukwu42@students.tntech.edu

Ordering Information
Quantity sales. Special discounts are available on quantity purchases by corporations, associations, and others.
For details, contact the "Special Sales Department" at the information above.

The Warrior's Weapons (Volume 2)
Dr. Uwakwe Christian Chukwu—1st edition
ISBN: 978-1-64606-336-9

Cover Design & Typesetting By
Divine Studios Inc
+1.678.599.7582

Printed By
Lan Manuel Print House
8700 Commerce Park Dr #111
Houston, Texas. 77036
Email: lmphhouston@gmail.com
Tel: +1.832.367.8420

Published in the United States of America

THE
WARRIOR'S
WEAPONS

••VOLUME TWO••

21 DAY SPIRITUAL WARFARE
PRAYER GUIDE

DR. UWAKWE C. CHUKWU

Dedication

To My Lovely Children:
Chiemelie, Onyinyechi, Mmesomachukwu, and Ebubechukwu.
Each of whom has a special place in my heart.
You are my little prayer warriors in our home.
You shall exceed your Dad!
God bless you all,
In Jesus name
Amen!

TABLE OF CONTENTS

Acknowledgment

My foremost gratitude goes to the Holy Spirit who provided the inspiration, guidance, and grace to write this book. I thank in a very special way Miss Marie Bernadette Abe Ewongkem for her editorial expertise in taking the manuscript of this book and meticulously moderating it. I am very thankful to you!

I am utterly grateful to my Spiritual Director and mentor, Rev. Fr. Cletus Imo. He is both my father and my model. His life inspires me much. It is largely his mentoring, combined with the support I receive from others like him that keep me aflame in the faith. A million thanks cannot suffice to express my gratitude to Rev. Fr. Anthony Madu for the sacrifices he makes in sharing the Word of God weekly in our Ministry.

Many words may be said, but none is enough to appreciate the support received from my parents, Mr. Nweke-Onovo Chukwu and Mrs. Roseline Chukwu, most especially for showing me the way to God. You have no idea of the gravity of my deeply-felt gratitude for your sacrifices that brought me thus far. Mum, you are the first prayer warrior I ever knew. You laid the foundation for my prayer life. You prayed the fire of God into my life!

I have no luxury of space to thank all the passionate and caring members of my ministry—*Hearts of Jesus and Mary Ministries* (HJM)—for their unrelenting prayers for my family and ministry. HJM family is a legion in my life, and I am filled with gratitude for their willingness in showering me with the greatest gift—prayers. I reserve a sincere gratitude to all the Board of Directors, Ministry Leaders, and Workers in the HJM Ministry, whose efforts in the ministry stir deep gratitude from my heart.

My gratitude goes to Mr. Emmanuel Aryee for taking his time to typeset this book and for designing the cover.

I am overwhelmingly grateful to my beautiful wife, Chinyere, and our wonderful children—Chiemelie, Onyinyechi, Mmesomachukwu, and Ebubechukwu—for making our family a happy home for all of us. This book is dedicated to the kids. I love you all, and may God bless you!

Preface

I wish to use this preface to set the stage for my readers as they get ready to read this book. Believers are at war with the kingdom of darkness. It is not, however, a war in which machines guns and bombers are used; it is, rather, a spiritual warfare in which spiritual weapons are used. There is war because the spiritual forces of darkness do not want the Kingdom of God to reign in the hearts of God's people. So, they weary God's children with attacks and temptations, hoping that they will yield to pressure. It cannot be overemphasized that Satan and his kingdom have some heinous agenda on the earth to oppose all that God stands for—and you are in the middle of that conflict!

Every day, people are feeling the effects of evil forces and yet, they don't know how to combat these evil forces. The spiritual war could be intense as to make even believers to wonder if actually there are redeemed by the Blood of Jesus Christ. Actually, you're primarily targeted by the enemy because you are redeemed—although there are other reasons why someone may be attacked (e.g. the anointing that you carry in you that you may not know about). You are now a threat to the kingdom of darkness, so the opposition against you increases.

Therefore, it is not enough for the believer to be redeemed. The believer should know how to fight with his/her spiritual weapons. He/she must be a warrior using his/her weapons to bind the forces of darkness, spoil their goods, pull down their strongholds, and cast down their wicked works. Once the believer has entered into this type of warfare, he/she can then claim back all what the devil has taken from him/her.

God has given us spiritual weapons of warfare to use in engaging the enemy in spiritual combats or conflicts. It is with these weapons that we can be able to recover our stolen blessings. God's weapons of warfare are unimaginably powerful!

This book, *The Warrior's Weapons,* takes you on a 21-day prayer program. Each chapter is divided into two parts: Part 1 and Part 2. It has a teaching component in Part 1 and a prayer session in Part 2. While the teaching component presents reflections aimed at acquiring spiritual knowledge on how to use the spiritual weapons, the prayer component presents warfare prayers devised to enable you to overtake the enemy with God's weapons. It has some inspiring stories to motivate you to expect your own testimonies. The book comes as a series.

This prayer manual will help you develop a proactive strategy to overthrow the enemy's agenda against your life. So prepare yourself for spiritual battles as God's warrior. I pray that this book brings out the warrior in you!

God bless you!

Uwakwe C. Chukwu
Simpsonville, South Carolina, USA
June, 2019

Introduction

"Stand, therefore, and fasten the belt of truth around your waist, and put on the breastplate of righteousness. As shoes for your feet put on whatever will make you ready to proclaim the Gospel of peace. With all of these, take the shield of faith, with which you will be able to quench all the flaming arrows of the evil one. Take the helmet of salvation, and the sword of the Spirit, which is the Word of God. Pray in the Spirit at all times in every prayer and supplication. To that end keep alert and always persevere in supplication for all the saints."

(Ephesians 6:14-18)

[Other suggested Bible passages to read: Psalm 91:11-12, 2 Chronicles 32:21, 2 Kings 19:35, Psalm 144:1, Revelation 12:11. 2 Chronicles 32:1-23, Isaiah 37:14–38, 2 Kings 18:17-37, 1 Samuel 17:45-47].

The footprints of man's spiritual enemy—the devil, the accuser of the brethren— are evident throughout history. Spiritual warfare is clearly spelled out as the ancient serpent draws his signature on the soil of humanity. In the Garden of Eden, he brought upon humanity the curse of death. In Bethlehem, he schemed to kill man's Savior, Jesus Christ. In the wilderness, he tempted man's Savior to abandon His mission to save us. In the Garden of Gethsemane, he set up a betrayal against the One who has come to save mankind. On the hills of Calvary, he manipulated the people to crucify Him to die on the

Cross, but on the third day, the devil's head was stomped as Jesus Christ resurrected gloriously.

The message is clear: Hell is ready to unleash fury against mankind, most especially the followers of Jesus Christ. Could this be the most appropriate time to remind us of the undeniable truth that the devil has come to steal, kill, and destroy (John 10:10)? We need to understand the seriousness of the spiritual war in which we are engaged. We ought to be armed and dangerous against every spiritual adversary. Yet, many believers live in denial, letting the enemy steal their blessings, destroy their relationship with Jesus, and kill their hope. But no more! It's time to put the enemy on notice!

Spiritual battle is real! As mentioned in Volume 1 of this book, you need God's weapons to fight a spiritual battle. You ought to take your spiritual weapons and armor very seriously and be made strong in the Lord. The weapons of God are effective. Only by using them, can we persevere in any spiritual conflict. Without them, we are like fodder for the forces of evil.

When you fight with God's weapons, what you are really doing is allowing God to fight for you – and, you know, when God fights, He never loses! God doesn't wound His enemies when He fights. He, rather, destroys them! When you fight with God's weapons, you will win because God is the one fighting it out. It is important to take note that God does not fight with weapons. In fact, He doesn't need weapons and armor. He Himself fights armor-free! However, we fight with God's armor and weapons, because we need them. That was why God gave them to us in the first place. While we engage in a spiritual battle with the weapons of our warfare, God endorses or approves of our prayer since we are praying His will.

Note in **2 Corinthians 10:4** that our spiritual weapons are *"Not carnal."* If we try to fight a spiritual battle with carnal weapons, we lose– and we lose every single time. The Bible tells us that *"by strength, no man shall prevail"* (1Samuel 2:9, NKJV). Examples of carnal weapons are intellect, prowess, power, beauty, physical strength, money, etc.

In this book, you have a prayer manual you need to become armed and dangerous against every adversary that threatens you and your destiny. With the passion and some insight I acquired from many years of being in the frontlines of spiritual warfare, I share with you—so as to equip you with —the Biblical weapons and practical strategies you need to battle the enemy successfully. With this book (as in other warfare books I have written), you would be able to discern and shut down the enemy's tactics, fight with your God-given authority, break free from destructive patterns, fortify your mind and heart against attacks, take back what the devil has stolen from you, and then mature in Christ and in spiritual warfare operations. Through the power of the Holy Spirit, who directed the writing of this book, you will be able to destroy the power of the enemy and protect all that God has given to you. This prayer manual places you in good stead for a unique role in this critical end time. The sweeping and the far-reaching effect shall be best described as awesome!

The need for spiritual weapons is heightened by the nature of spiritual war. You are not fighting one person, but a well-organized kingdom. The manner with which you engage in a fight against one person is not the same way you fight a group of people who are all out to fight you. This concern is amplified when the group coming to fight you is a gang of spiritual ruffians fully armed to kill you. This picture is a miniature when we consider that in spiritual warfare, it is a kingdom coming after you to kill, destroy, or at the least to take away your blessings (John 10:10).

Although spiritual warfare is the Kingdom of God against the kingdom of darkness, you are alone in this battle if you do not fight with God's weapons. How do you describe the pitifulness of someone alone in a demonic conflict? He will come out of it the day an ant survives a fight with an elephant! The life of the demoniac whose story is narrated in **Luke 8:26-40** is the perfect picture of a destiny helplessly alone and trapped in the devil's deep sea. The wickedness of the devil and his kingdom on this young man is the way it goes when the kingdom of darkness fights a person.

As we know very well, there are two spiritual kingdoms. Each kingdom is ruled by one lord or master. These kingdoms stand in sharp opposition to one another. These kingdoms are God's kingdom of Light and Satan's kingdom of darkness. The conflict between these two kingdoms is fierce. The struggle we go through is due to an affliction from the kingdom of darkness. The enemy has to be disarmed and overthrown before we can be free. This is possible only by praying with God's spiritual weapons given to us. So, use the weapons that God has given you!

You have the personal responsibility to utilize the divine might to fight back the forces of darkness. When will you decide to bind the strongman that is holding your hands back and taking the spoils (**Matthew 12:29**). Claim back your family for the Lord Jesus Christ! It does not matter how long your people have been in captivity.

You get results when you begin to pray like a warrior with your weapons. The proof of the effectiveness of praying with this book (your God-given weapon) is the inner witness I have that God will grant His people the grace to experience numerous deliverances, healings, and miracles.

Therefore, this book is structured to lead you through a 21-day fasting and prayer program against your spiritual enemies using your God-given weapons. It is strongly recommended that you engage in this prayer program using the prayer structure presented in Table 1.

Table 1

A 21 – DAY PRAYER PROGRAM USING THIS BOOK.

DAY	CHAPTER TO STUDY AND PRAY WITH	FASTING PERIOD
Day 1	Introduction	12:00am - 1:00pm
Day 2	Chapter 1: The Anointing (Part 1)	
Day 3	Chapter 1: The Anointing (Part 2)	
Day 4	Chapter 2: Praise and Worship (Part 1)	
Day 5	Chapter 2: Praise and Worship (Part 2)	
Day 6	Chapter 3: Our Confessions and Declarations (Part 1)	
Day 7	Chapter 3: Our Confessions and Declarations (Part 2)	
Day 8	Chapter 4: Our Testimony (Par-t 1)	12:00am- 3:00pm
Day 9	Chapter 4: Our Testimony (Part 2)	
Day 10	Chapter 5: Praying in Tongues (Part 1)	
Day 11	Chapter 5: Praying in Tongues (Part 2)	
Day 12	Chapter 6: Praying with the Elements (Part 1)	
Day 13	Chapter 6: Praying with the Elements (Part 2)	
Day 14	Chapter 7: The Authority of the Believer (Part 1)	
Day 15	Chapter 7: The Authority of the Believer (Part 2)	
Day 16	Chapter 8: Knowledge (Part 1)	
Day 17	Chapter 8: Knowledge (Part 2)	
Day 18	Chapter 9: Agreement Prayer (Part 1)	
Day 19	Chapter 9: Agreement Prayer (Part 2)	12:00am to 6:00pm
Day 20	Chapter 10: Faith (Part 1)	
Day 21	Chapter 10: Faith (Part 2)	

This book invites you to pray *"The Warrior's Prayer"* because you are Christ's warrior. You will be making this prayer daily throughout the 21 days of this prayer program.

The Warrior's Prayer

"Heavenly Father,
Your warrior prepares for battle.
Today I claim victory over Satan
By putting on the whole armor of God!
"I put on the Girdle of Truth!
May I stand firm in the truth of Your Word
So I will not be a victim of Satan's lies.
"I put on the Breastplate of Righteousness!
May it guard my heart from evil
So I will remain pure and holy,
Protected under the Most Precious Blood of Jesus Christ.
"I put on the Shoes of Peace!
May I stand firm in the Good News of the Gospel
So Your peace will shine
Through me and be a light to all I encounter.
"I take the Shield of Faith!
May I be ready for Satan's fiery darts of doubt,
denial, and deceit
So I will not be vulnerable to a spiritual defeat.
"I put on the Helmet of Salvation!
May I keep my mind focused on You
So Satan will not have a stronghold on my thoughts.
"I take the Sword of the Spirit!
May the two-edged sword of Your Word be ready in my hands
So I can expose the tempting words of Satan.
By faith, your warrior has put on the whole armor of God!
I am prepared to live this day in spiritual victory.
Amen!"

—**Unknown Author**

Spiritual communion with Christ is also an integral part of this prayer exercise. Spiritual communion is a practice of desiring union with Jesus Christ in the Holy Eucharist. Although this prayer may be used to prepare our hearts before receiving Holy Communion, it is also used by individuals who cannot receive Communion. Therefore, we shall be making the prayer of *"The Act of Spiritual Communion"* during the 21 days prayer program. Remember, however, that you can make this prayer from anywhere you might happen to be, at any time, day or night. It is a simple but powerful prayer to recharge your spirit and conquer the enemies! Therefore, brethren, it behooves you to use this prayer daily!

The Act of Spiritual Communion

"My Jesus, I believe that You are present in the
Most Holy Sacrament.
I love You above all things, and I desire to receive
You into my soul.
Since I cannot at this moment receive You sacramentally,
come at least spiritually into my heart.
I embrace You as if You were already there
and unite myself wholly to You.
Never permit me to be separated from You.
Amen!"

–**St. Alphonsus Liguori**

Note:

- This book is written to all of you who acknowledge that there is a battle and who seek a way out. And if you dismiss the notion of spiritual warfare, then I suggest you ask God in prayer to enlighten you. Keep this book handy for when this battle is revealed to you, you will find it a gold in your hand.

- If you are a Catholic, you are encouraged to consider receiving the Sacraments of reconciliation (confession) and Holy Communion either during or before you begin praying using this book.

DAY 1 - Warfare Prayers

1. Praise and worship God as the Holy Spirit leads you.

2. Pray **Psalm 51** for the forgiveness of your sins.
   a. Gracious Lord Jesus, forgive me for the ways I have given the enemy an opportunity to attack me. Cleanse me with Your Most Precious Blood;
   b. Help me to submit anew today to Your authority, control, and will;
   c. Lord Jesus, help me to take back every lost territory the devil has taken from me.

3. Pray **Psalm 144** for security and deliverance from the spiritual enemies.

4. Put on the full armor of God using *"The Warrior's Prayer"* (see the prayer as above).

5. Pray *"The Act of Spiritual Communion"* prayer (see the prayer as above).

6. I stand against Satan's attempts to outwit or keep me from using my spiritual weapons of warfare effectively, in the name of Jesus Christ.

7. Jeremiah 33:3 says, *"Call to me and I will answer you."* Make the following prayers in the name of Jesus Christ:
   a. Talk to God about the situations you are passing through. Ask Him to help you;
   b. Talk to God about the troubles other people are going through in their lives *(ask the Holy Spirit to bring their needs to your mind for you to pray for them)*.
      i. Ask Him to help them at their places of need. Let God help them to align with His will for them;
      ii. May they suit up in God's armor and experience victory by His power.
   c. Pray for the Church, especially that She stands *"Against the wiles of the devil"* (Ephesians 6:11).
      i. Pray that Christians *"Put on the whole armor of God"* (Ephesians 6:11);
      ii. Pray that the fire of God's love shall be flaming in the Church;
      iii. Pray for global revival;
      iv. Pray for the Ministers of God to be on fire.
   d. Pray for the Society and social institutions (schools, hospitals, prisons, etc.).

8. Lord Jesus Christ, help me to daily and fully use my weapons of warfare to stand against the enemy's wicked schemes—in the name of Jesus Christ.

9. Lord Jesus Christ, in using the weapons of warfare, help me to keep my mind fixed on what is true, noble, right, pure, lovely, admirable, excellent, and praiseworthy **(Philippians 4:8)** —in the name of Jesus Christ.

10. Thank You, Lord Jesus Christ, for the spiritual weapons and armor you have given us to fight spiritual battles: the belt of truth, breastplate of righteousness, helmet of salvation, feet fitted with the readiness to proclaim the Gospel of peace, shield of faith, and the sword of the Spirit, the Word of God **(Ephesians 6:10-18).**

    a. Thank You, Lord Jesus, for I need each piece of those weapons to stay strong in Your mighty power;

    b. Thank You, Lord Jesus, for such spiritual weapons as faith, truth, and righteousness that demolish strongholds.

II. I cover this prayer with the Most Precious Blood of Jesus Christ (7 times).

Chapter 1

The Anointing

"The yoke shall be destroyed because of the anointing."
(Isaiah 10:27)

"God anointed Jesus of Nazareth with the Holy Spirit and with power."
(Acts 10:38)

[Other suggested Bible passages to read:
Isaiah 10:27, Acts 10:38, Luke 4:18-19,
Mark 16:17-18, Isaiah 61:1-3].

DAY 2 - Part I: Reflection

Why do shepherds anoint the heads of their sheep with oil? Sheep are easy targets for flies, lice, and ticks. When a sheep's head is not covered with oil, it becomes easily attacked by these blood-sucking pests. Bugs would crawl into the ear canal of the unoiled sheep, eating away at it, creating a serious nuisance and causing terrible pain. The pain from the bugs would be so severe on the sheep that the sheep would bang his skull on rocks and against trees to ease its suffering. Over time, the sheep stands the risk of breaking his own skull in the process.

When God offers to anoint us with His oil, it means He offers us protection from the "parasites" of this world. These "parasites" symbolically represent all that seek to eat away at us: sickness, addictions, depression, and so on! If we hide from God, we become unoiled. We become victims of the devil's spiritual parasites. We become weighed down with the burdens that God could easily remove from us. In a sense, we become so filled with pain that we "hit our heads against the rocks" of this world. Many have "hit their heads on the rock" of drugs in the bid to seek relief from their suffering.

God's oil keeps away the "bugs" from attacking us. For this reason, God anoints His people with oil just as the shepherds anoint the heads of their sheep with oil. The Psalmist attests to this fact when he said of God, *"you anoint my head with oil"* **(Psalm 23:5).**

Many believers are not aware that the anointing of the Holy Spirit is one of our secret weapons of spiritual warfare against the devil. The exploits of Samson were not by calling upon the name of Jesus Christ or His Blood, and definitely not by calling the Fire of God to come down like Elijah did, nor did he confess with his mouth or profess the Word of God; not by praise, fasting, praying in tongues or praying with the elements— but by the power of anointing. All that Samson did was not possible by his own strength but by the anointing of the Holy Spirit as *"The Spirit of the Lord came mightily upon him"* **(Judges 15:14).** One of the tragedies of our time is that so many Christians are not walking in their anointing.

The anointing you carry is a powerful weapon of warfare! Even Jesus Christ had to be anointed to confront the spiritual forces he dealt with in His Ministry works—thus He testifies in Luke 4:18 as thus: *"The Spirit of the Lord is upon me because He has anointed me... to let the oppressed go free."* Anointing was evident by the miracles that Jesus performed and the lives that He touched. No evil presence can withstand the Power of the anointing that flowed from Jesus Christ. We know that *"The Son of God was revealed for this purpose, to destroy the works of the devil"* **(1 John 3:8).**

The anointing in Jesus destroys every yoke of bondage. Jesus is the embodiment of the Power of the Anointing! Anointing is infinitely so powerful that it brings freedom, liberty, and deliverance to the captives. And guess what? That anointing is available to empower you to do great exploits in the Kingdom of God! Anointing is a powerful force on the earth!

It takes anointing to break the yoke of oppression and *"release to the captives"* (Luke 4:18c). Scripture testifies to this saying, *"The yoke shall be destroyed because of the anointing"* (Isaiah 10:27). It is the anointing in the Pool of Bethesda that healed people as *"An angel went down ... into the pool, and troubled the water"* (John 5:4).

The Holy Spirit is the Yoke-Breaker; the anointing of the Holy Spirit breaks all the 'yoke" the devil puts on us—be it sickness, diseases, bad habits, fear, or poverty. The "yoke" breaks and its imposed limitations are lifted when we choose to walk under the power of the anointing. **Isaiah 59:19** says, *"When the enemy shall come in like a flood, the Spirit of the Lord shall lift up a standard against him."*

As the ropes tying Samson began to break like a thread when his anointing was stirred (**Judges 16:12**), so anointing completely breaks all the chains of bondage in our lives as we stir the anointing of the Holy Spirit in us. The advice of Paul to Timothy (in **2 Timothy 1:6**) to stir his gifts into flame is as well a fitting admonition for us.

The bottom line is that the fire of the anointing must be kept burning in our lives. Your anointing works when you walk on the path of your anointing. Your anointing was not meant to sit unused on a shelf, but to be living and active, working in the trenches of your life. Don't forget: *"you have been anointed by the Holy One"* (1 John 2:20). Yes, God says that you are anointed by Him. Is it not time to take our anointing off the shelf and use it? Keep your anointing on fire!

The anointing stirs, sharpens, and spiritually activates our spiritual senses—our eyes open to see in the spirit and our ears tuned to the frequencies of heaven to know Heaven's strategies to employ in fighting the enemy. For instance, Elisha's spiritual eyes had to open for him to see a troop of God's Angels surrounding his estate when the Arameans came to attack him (2 Kings 6:8-23). He then prayed to God for the Arameans to become blind. This was his prayer: *"'Strike this people, please, with blindness.' So He struck them with blindness as Elisha had asked"* (2 Kings 6:18). Elisha understands that his enemies are crippled when they cannot see.

The subject of activating the anointing for spiritual wars can only be scratched at the surface in this book as this is a whole department of warfare operations. The flow of anointing is necessary for spiritual combat, and the absence of it is a serious limitation to the successful engagement of the enemy in spiritual warfare.

Just like all opponents come after the man carrying the ball in a football match, so the enemy targets people that carry anointing. For this reason, Jezebel targeted to kill Prophet Elijah, Delilah came after Samson, and Herodias after John the Baptist. The devil has a deep hatred for people who carry prophetic destiny! He wants them dead! Most people carry powerful anointing but they don't know. Usually, such people experience high gravity of attacks. Often, they wonder why they have to suffer from all the troubles that they go through in life.

Anointing attracts troubles and attacks— but God promises to deliver His anointed from all of them (Psalm 34:19). King David's troubles started after Prophet Samuel anointed him King of Israel. Was it not *"When the Philistines heard that David had been anointed King over Israel, [that] all the Philistines went up in search of David; but David heard about it and went down to the stronghold"* (2 Samuel 5:17).

You see, before the oil of anointing came upon David, nobody cared about him, but not after! Your anointing can single you out for the spiritual enemies to go in search of you. However, when the enemies come after you, the anointing is stirred to protect you. The other day, the Prophet Elijah's anointing was stirred when two bands of fifty men came to arrest him, and the result was fire coming down from Heaven **(2 Kings 1:9-15)**. Stir your anointing into flame!

LET US PRAY!

1. Reflect on how this reflection on *"The Anointing"* ministers to you.

2. Pray and ask God for the forgiveness of your sins using **Psalm 51.**

3. Put on the full armor of God using *"The Warrior's Prayer"* (see page 16).

4. Pray *"The Act of Spiritual Communion"* prayer (see page 17).

5. Pray **Psalm 23** (pay attention to verse 5: *"You anoint my head with oil; my cup overflows"*).

6. Holy Spirit, I pray that You will fall upon me now in the same way that You fell upon the Apostles, in the name of Jesus Christ.

7. Prayer for divine activation of your anointing *(pray in the name of Jesus Christ)*. Holy Spirit, please activate...
   a. My spiritual womb for the conception of miracles;
   b. My spiritual wings to fly above limitations like an eagle;
   c. My hands to prosper in every endeavor;
   d. My feet to possess the blessings of the land;
   e. My legs to walk in dominion;
   f. My eyes to see the glory of God;

g. My ears to hear clearly in the spirit;

h. My heart to love and treasure God;

i. My soul to receive divine knowledge;

j. My tongue to become *"like a sharp razor"* (Psalm 52:2);

k. My mouth to speak forth the fire of prophetic utterances;

l. My lips to declare Your praise (Psalm 51:15);

m. My body for divine healing;

n. My body, soul, and spirit to carry the garment of fire;

o. My brain and mind to be saturated with the Word of God;

p. My hands to war and my fingers to fight (Psalm 144:1);

q. My loins for the rivers of the Living water to flow (John 7:38);

r. My thoughts to think only of God;

s. My life for divine favor;

t. My destiny to attract divine appointments and open doors of opportunities;

u. My prayer Altar to become an Altar of fire;

v. My ways to align perfectly with God's will;

w. My days for good times and blessed moments;

x. My divine office for miraculous overflows;

y. My dreams for prophetic revelations;

z. My prophetic keys to unlock heaven for release of blessings.

8. I decree that my head will never lack fresh oil of anointing, in the name of Jesus Christ. In the name of Jesus Christ, I decree that:

   a. This oil acts as a seal of approval upon my life;

   b. This oil endorses me, equips me, empowers me, and makes rooms for me;

   c. This oil causes me to live in the overflow of grace;

   d. This oil ushers me into my prophetic destiny.

9. Thank the Lord Jesus Christ and cover this prayer with His Most Precious Blood (7 times).

DAY 3 - Part II: Warfare Prayers

Note:

- The anointing of God resides inside of you. Use it and stir the anointing!

- Ask God to help you walk in a stronger anointing.

- The road to deliverance from the enemy's shackles requires the flow of the anointing.

1. Anointing begins to flow as we burst spontaneously into some songs that portray the Anointing of the Holy Spirit. Such songs change the spiritual climate and set the stage ready to bring freedom, liberty, and deliverance to the captives. Let the Holy Spirit lead you into songs that will activate the power of the anointing.

2. Use **Psalm 51** to ask God for the forgiveness of your sins. The Blood of Jesus Christ cleanses me from all sin (**1 John 1:7**).

3. Put on the full armor of God using *"The Warrior's Prayer"* (see page 16).

4. Pray *"The Act of Spiritual Communion"* prayer (see page 17).

5. Holy Spirit, I pray that You use this prayer to activate divine intervention in every area of my life, in the name of Jesus Christ.

6. I speak that God's anointing destroys every yoke in my life and that my soul, spirit, and body now function in order according to divine systems of protocol—in the name of Jesus Christ.

7. As God's anointed, I decree that *(pray in the name of Jesus Christ)*:

    a. No evil power can stop me from walking on the path of my anointing as I make this prayer;

    b. God's plans and purposes for my life and over my family shall stand.

8. As God's anointed, I arise to establish my legal right and dominion over this region and over every territory which God has given me a jurisdictional authority, in the name of Jesus Christ.

9. In the name of Jesus Christ, Whose anointed I am and whom I serve, I decree that as I make this prayer, every knee must bow and every tongue confess that Jesus Christ is Lord **(Philippians 2:10-11)**.

10. I place upon myself the armor of God's Anointing as I take on *(pray in the name of Jesus Christ):*
    a. Truth to cover my loins;
    b. The breastplate of righteousness to cover my heart and chest area;
    c. The Gospel of peace to cover my feet
    d. The shield of faith to defensively and offensively cover my body;
    e. The helmet of salvation to cover my head
    f. The sword of the Spirit (the Word of God) for my protection;
    g. The robe of righteousness for living in righteousness.

11. I decree that as my anointing is stirred, I am released from demonic cycles, seasons, calendars, and timetables, in the name of Jesus Christ.

12. By God's anointing upon my life, I dislodge and destroy demonic anchors that keep me in old cycles — the cycle of poverty, hardship, lack, struggle, chronic sickness, and diseases—in the name of Jesus Christ.

13. As the ropes tying Samson began to break like a thread when his anointing was stirred **(Judges 16:12)**, so shall God's anointing upon my life be stirred, causing every chain of bondage tying me or my loved ones to be broken, in the name of Jesus Christ (*spend some time here praying*).

14. I shall stir my gifts into flame **(2 Timothy 1:6)**, in the name of Jesus Christ. Pray the following in the name of Jesus Christ:
    a. The fire of my anointing must be burning in me always;
    b. My anointing shall not sit unused.

15. Lord Jesus Christ, open my spiritual eyes to see what my natural eyes cannot see, in the name of Jesus Christ.
    a. Remove every spiritual distraction and the scales that have blinded me from seeing clearly in the spirit;
    b. Let me see into the spirit realm with understanding;
    c. Holy Spirit, help me discern the things that I see but do not understand;
    d. Bless my eyes to see every entrapment of the evil one that is trying to come against me.

16. Begin to confess the following in the name of Jesus Christ:
    a. I am very glad that I am anointed;
    b. My anointing distinguishes me;
    c. My anointing destroys the works of the devil;
    d. My anointing shall heal, set the oppressed free, and bring people to salvation;
    e. My anointing shall increase mightily;
    f. No unclean spirit or agent of the devil shall contaminate my anointing;
    g. **1 John 2:20** confirms that I *"have been anointed by the Holy One"*;
    h. I am a threat to the kingdom of darkness because of the anointing I carry in me— Amen! Amen! Amen!

17. As I pray, anointing flows freely in me, in the name of Jesus Christ. Therefore, as the anointing flows (praying in the name of Jesus Christ):
    a. Standing on **Isaiah 40:4**
        i. Every valley must be brought up;
        ii. Every mountain must be made low;
        iii. Every crooked place must be made straight;
        iv. Every rough path must be smoothened.
    b. I receive the strategies and divine tactics to move all spiritual mountains, psychological mountains, relational mountains, and political mountains—in the name of Jesus Christ;
    c. I break through that which is insurmountable and impenetrable.
        i. I command prisons and walls to come down;
        ii. I break through impenetrable walls and barricades into the realm of the miraculous;
        iii. I break into the realm of increase, supernatural reservoir, and divine turnaround;
        iv. I bulldoze my way past demonic gatekeepers;
        v. I cut asunder the gates of brass and the bars of iron.
    d. I advance past stubborn problems and situations;
    e. Spiritual embargoes placed on my destiny are lifted.

18. Call on the anointing to come on you with power, authority, and dominion. Pray in the name of Jesus Christ:

    a. Holy Spirit, I pray that you anoint us with all what we need today to set the captives free to your Glory.
        i. I pray for greater gifts of spiritual discernment;
        ii. I pray for Word of wisdom, revelation gifts, and the gift of Knowledge.
    b. I pray that You use this prayer to deliver those who cannot deliver themselves.

19. I decree that the glory of God is my reward, in the name of Jesus Christ.

20. Lord Jesus Christ, I thank You for the anointing over my life. Thank You for teaching me how to use my anointing to live victoriously.

21. I cover this prayer with the Most Precious Blood of Jesus Christ (7 times).

Chapter 2

Praise and Worship

"Who is like unto thee, O Lord, among the gods? who is like thee, glorious in holiness, fearful in praises, doing wonders?"

(Exodus 15:11 KJV)

[Other suggested Bible passages to read:
2 Chronicles 20:5-30, Psalm 66:1–2, 1 Chronicles 16:34-36,
Acts 16:25-28, Psalm 136:1-26].

DAY 4 - Part I: Reflection

Jacob gave a prophetic blessing to Judah saying that Judah was to be a praise and to have victory over his enemies **(Genesis 49:8)**. Therefore, Jacob's last words to his son, Judah, reveals to us the connection between praise and victory over the enemies.

Praise and worship are powerful weapons in deliverance and spiritual warfare operations. As you begin to sing, praise, and worship the Lord, the spiritual climate begins to change as the glory of God comes down to inhabit the praises of His people **(Psalm 22:3)**. The demons on assignment in the environment where there is praise and worship are thrown into confusion.

You have no clue of what happens in the spirit realm when your praise and worship go up to the Lord. The Scripture gives us a clue in **Acts 16:26** that as Paul and Silas were praising God in the midnight, *"Suddenly there was such a violent earthquake that the* *foundations of the prison were shaken."* Do you see that? Look, demons can't stand the atmosphere of praise and worship. They simply cannot function. Praise and worship torment evil spirits! I have seen it paralyze the devil!

Wait a minute: What did the people do to deliver King Saul when he was afflicted by an evil spirit? Rushed to a Mental Health Clinic? No! Do you think he was given some anti-depression pills to calm him down? No!! So what did they do to cast the evil spirit in the King? Praise!!! The only thing they did to help the King was to call on David, the praise master. As David began to play on his harp and sing praises to his God, the evil spirit simply departed from King Saul (1 Samuel 16:14-23). That's how powerful and effective praise is!

You see, the people of the Old Testament didn't have the name of Jesus Christ as a weapon, but they did have praise and worship. Their worship panaches were sacrifice and praise—and the results were amazing. We see the Old Testament praise-culture in the Book of Psalms. They went to the battlefields with praise— for instance, King Jehoshaphat went into battle with praise (2 Chronicles 20:5-30).

Nobody sends the choir out first in a battle—unless it's a really bad choir and you want to get rid of them! Why send the choir out first and believe you're going to win? You probably think that King Jehoshaphat was out of his mind, but his decision further validates praise as a powerful weapon in spiritual warfare. The result was utter confusion in the enemy's camp, a confusion that caused the enemies to kill themselves, leaving their treasures for the Israelites to harvest.

> *"As they began to sing and praise, the Lord set an ambush against the Ammonites, Moab, and Mount Seir, who had come against Judah, so that they were routed. For the Ammonites and Moab attacked the inhabitants of Mount Seir, destroying them utterly; and when they*

had made an end of the inhabitants of Seir, they all helped to destroy one another...they were corpses lying on the ground; no one had escaped. When Jehoshaphat and his people came to take the booty from them, they found livestock in great numbers, goods, clothing, and precious things, which they took for themselves until they could carry no more. They spent three days taking the booty, because of its abundance"

(2 Chronicles 20:22-25)

My dear, are you aware that your praise can force the tyrant strongman to drop every of your inheritance held hostage for ages? Has it crossed your mind that demonic chains break in the atmosphere of praise? Well, I wish to remind you that it was as Paul and Silas praised God in the prison that *"At once, all the prison doors flew open, and everyone's chains came loose"* (Acts 16:26).

Praise can be the artillery barrage that softens up the enemy for the frontal assault of the Word as you pray with the Word in warfare. Most demons get expelled from people (or severely weakened) during praise and worship session, quite before the actual deliverance starts. Praise and worship soften the ground for deliverance as they make it easier to cast out demons. In fact, it is the right thing to add the elements of praise and worship in the middle of spiritual warfare, whether during deliverance session or during general warfare engagements.

If you are facing a prolonged battle in your life, it is appropriate that you worship and praise the Lord right through it – even if you do not feel like doing so. As you do this, the Holy Spirit will then rise up in you, and you will feel His peace and joy running through you. Then you will realize that He will help you handle it and get through it. A tremendous move of God begins to happen when people fully surrender their entire problems into God's hands in the atmosphere of praise.

Why have we overlooked and underused the weapon of praise to rout the enemy? I hope, like Jehoshaphat, you will from now on use your weapon of praise as your warfare style to confront those tyrants against you—and in doing so, you shall see God shake the grip of wickedness out of your atmosphere.

LET US PRAY!

1. Reflect on how this reflection on *"Shouts of Praise, Singing & Worship"* ministers to you.

2. Pray and ask God for the forgiveness of your sins using **Psalm 51.**

3. Put on the full armor of God using *"The Warrior's Prayer"* (see page 16).

4. Pray *"The Act of Spiritual Communion"* prayer (see page 17).

5. Pray **Psalm 145** (a psalm of praise).

6. Lord Jesus Christ, may I daily give you praise in the sanctuary of my heart. You are my All—in the name of Jesus Christ!

7. Now begin to praise our Lord Jesus Christ:
    a. Praise Him for His grace **(Ephesians 1:6)**;
    b. Praise Him for His goodness **(Psalm 135:3)**;
    c. Praise Him for His kindness **(Psalm 117)**;
    d. Praise Him for His salvation **(Ephesians 2:8-9)**;
    e. Praise Him for His holiness, mercy, and justice **(Psalm 99:3-4)**;
    f. Bless His Holy name **(Psalm 103:1)**.

8. Now begin to praise Jesus Christ. Freely continue to praise Him saying: I praise You, Lord Jesus, You are -------- (*Use the following praises or any other praise the Holy Spirit might put into your mouth*).

- Our Victory
- The Lord of lords
- The Mighty Warrior
- The Name above all names
- Our Strength
- King of creation
- My Hiding place
- The Destroyer of rebel spirits
- The Savior of the world
- The only Holy One
- The Living Waters
- The living Word
- The Great High Priest
- The Rock of all ages
- The Way, the Truth, and Life
- The Wonderful Counselor
- The Fountain of   Holiness
- The Everlasting One
- The Most High God
- The Just Judge
- Our Covenant keeping God
- Emmanuel, God with us
- Our Foundation
- Our Healer
- All that I Need
- The Lamb of God
- Our Salvation

- All that I want to be
- The Redeemer
- The Almighty God
- Our Deliverer
- My Defense
- The King of kings
- The Winner
- Christ, the King
- The Lion of Judah
- My Provider
- Our Fortress
- The Light of the World
- The Bread of Life
- The Messiah
- The Good Shepherd
- The Lord of Hosts
- The Great I am that I am
- The Mountain Refuge
- Our Righteousness
- Our Sanctifier
- The Resurrection & the Life
- The beginning & the End
- The only Hope of Salvation
- Worthy of all praise
- The Cornerstone
- The Promise of the Father
- The Alpha & the Omega

9. Go on offering God some praise and worship songs *(at least 15mins)*.

10. Thank the Lord Jesus Christ and cover this prayer with His Most Precious Blood (7 times).

DAY 5 - Part II: Warfare Prayers

Note:

- God does want us to be able to worship and praise Him. And nothing will touch the heart of God more than if you start to worship and praise Him right in the middle of a severe storm cloud. As you begin to praise God, you witness the devil's agenda against you de-programmed, while God installs His Divine agenda for you. Praise opens the floodgates of Heaven. So, ambush the enemy with your praise!

- Be singing songs of praise intermittently as you proceed in this prayer.

1. Anointing begins to flow as we burst spontaneously into some songs that portray the Anointing of the Holy Spirit. Such songs change the spiritual climate, set the stage ready to bring freedom, liberty, and deliverance to the captives. Let the Holy Spirit lead you into songs that activate the anointing.

2. Use **Psalm 51** to ask God for the forgiveness of your sins. The Blood of Jesus Christ cleanses me from all sin **(1 John 1:7)**.

3. Put on the full armor of God using *"The Warrior's Prayer"* (see page 16).

4. Pray *"The Act of Spiritual Communion"* prayer (see page 17).

5. I decree that the environment of this place is sanctified with the Blood of Jesus Christ, in the name of Jesus Christ. Therefore, in the name of Jesus Christ:
   a. I take authority over satanic atmospheres and climates created by cultic activities, incantations, witchcraft projections, violence, and so on;
   b. I command the ..... (*pick from the following list*) climate to shift right now for the King of Glory, Lord Jesus Christ, to be enthroned—in the name of Jesus Christ.

- Spiritual
- Economic
- Social
- Cultural
- Educational
- Political
- Ecclesiastical

c. I resist all territorial strongholds and prison gates.

6. I decree that as I praise God, I will swiftly drift and ascend into the realm of the supernatural and will not be earthbound, in the name of Jesus Christ. Therefore, in the name of Jesus Christ:
   a. I advance into new supernatural levels, new dimensions, new realms, and new territories for breakthrough and miracles to occur;
   b. The anointing of God breaks every yoke and opens every spiritual gateway;
   c. Angels are assigned to reinforce me;
   d. I tap into the Apostolic and Prophetic veins;
   e. The floodgates of heaven are opened.

7. As I praise God, let there be fire in my mouth as I advance in this prayer, in the name of Jesus Christ.

8. As I praise God, the atmosphere is filled with the Glory of God. I declare that the atmosphere is now suitable for ..... (*pick from the following list*) to thrive right now, in the name of Jesus Christ.

- My family
- My loved ones
- My Prayer life
- My Ministry
- My relationships
- My finances
- My business
- My ideas
- My nation
- The Government

9. As I praise God, the power of the God of Joshua is manifesting and causing every impenetrable wall to fall down, in the name of Jesus Christ. Continue with the following prayers: in the name of Jesus Christ, as I praise God...
   a. All satanic barriers, blockages, barricades, and embargoes are lifted right now;

b. All spiritual bars and iron membranes are smashed into irreparable pieces.

10. As I praise God, I declare that all satanic gadgets and communication lines set up to frustrate the plans and purposes of my life are interrupted, in the name of Jesus Christ.

11. As I praise God, all satanic firebrands are extinguished and all diabolical cycles reversed, in the name of Jesus Christ.

12. As I praise God, I am released from unprofitable living, in the name of Jesus Christ.

13. In **Psalm 69:30-33,** David turned from complaint and misery to praising God. As David climbed out of the pit of misery through praise, so I am walking out of every ugly situation that I find myself through praise to God—in the name of Jesus Christ.

14. Go on offering God some praise and worship songs (at least 15mins).

15. After a long period of waiting for deliverance, David, in the end, praised God with thanksgiving songs as God has answered Him, putting a new song in his mouth **(Psalm 40:1-3).** Now, begin to thank the Lord Jesus Christ for answering your prayers and sacrifice of praises.
    a. Lord Jesus, I thank You for the power of praise and worship;
    b. Lord Jesus, I thank You for teaching me how praise and worship are weapons for living a victorious life.

16. I cover this prayer with the Most Precious Blood of Jesus Christ (7 times).

Chapter 3

Our Confessions and Declarations

"Death and life are in the power of the tongue, and those who love it will eat its fruits"
(Proverbs 18:21)

"You will also declare a thing, and it will be established for you"
(Job 22:28, NKJV).

[Other suggested Bible passages to read:
James 3:3-5, Psalm 118:17, Philippians 4:19, Philippians 4:13,
Philippians 1:6, Deuteronomy 28:6, 3 John 1:2,
Isaiah 40:31, Psalm 34:10].

DAY 6 - Part I: Reflection

Speech is one of the greatest gifts which liken man to his Creator, whose Word is all powerful. Our words are powerful too! Our words can change our world and shape our future. The words we speak can make or mar us—*"for by your words you will be justified, and by your words, you will be condemned"* (Matthew 12:37). More so, what you say about yourself has a greater impact on you than anything anybody else says about you. Do you know that *"You are snared by the utterance of your lips, [and] caught by the words of your mouth"?* (Proverbs 6:2).

Was it not when the people sent to spy the Promised Land came back confessing negatively, saying *"to ourselves we seemed like grasshoppers, and so we seemed to them"* (Numbers 13:33) that the Lord said to them, *"I will do to you the very things I heard you say"* (Numbers 14:28). With their mouth, they chose to be like grasshoppers before their enemies—and so they were. Was it not when Esau—very hungry and in need of eating Jacob's stew—that he confessed with his mouth saying, *"I am about to die; of what use is a birthright to me?"* that he *"sold his birthright to Jacob"* (Genesis 25:29-34)?

In fact, there is power in the confessions of our mouths. Our words have the power to stop our victory from occurring. Our words also have the power to unlock the chains that have dragged us down. One of the ways you can break free from the strongholds of defeated mentality is simply by declaring and confessing words of victory. In fact, we are the words we speak every day!

Demonic spirits can go into operations against you by using the negative words of your mouth against you. Was it not when Joab declared with his mouth saying, *"No, I will die here"* even though he was at the place of safety that Solomon ordered his death by the hand of Benaiah saying, *"Do as he has said, strike him down and bury him"* (1 Kings 2:29-34)?

I once met a man in an amusement park having a good time. In the course of our discussion, he told me that he has cancer and would soon go home. He said it casually with smiles as if he would soon go home to sleep and come back to the amusement park the next day for another fun. I was startled when he clarified that *"I would soon go home"* meant he would soon die!

So, I requested to pray for him. To this, he gave me a shock of my life saying, *"O thank you! I am 54; that's a good number, not bad, you know."* Evidently, this man does not see life beyond 54 years. His words betray the faith to rise out from the ashes of hopelessness. He does not see himself growing stronger, living a long, healthy, and happy life. He settled for what the Doctor told him, instead of wrestling his case with prayer for a change of story.

Poor folk! He signed his death sentence and took his package by his confessions! The package will now belong to him legally and Satan can now enforce the package on him. Immediately you say, *"I am sick,"* you have signed a package. The Jews signed a package the moment they said, *"His Blood be on us and on our children!"* (Matthew 27:25).

How many have condemned themselves by the words of their mouths!

The devil is a bad postmaster, you know! He will put the stamps of condemnation on whoever confesses negative words with his/her mouth. It is very sad that a lot of people kill themselves every day and accept evil packages with their mouths. Stop signing your death warrant, my friend!

You need to know that you can arrest the demonic forces by the words of your mouth—O yes! This is one reason why your confession is important. Has the weak confessed, *"I am strong"* (Joel 3:10)? Job 22:29 says, *"When men are cast down, then you shall say, there is lifting up"* (AKJV). On this premise, the Lord assures us: *"I will do to you the very things I heard you say"* (Numbers 14:28). Was it not as soon as Joshua declared with his mouth saying, *"Sun, stand still at Gibeon, and Moon, in the valley of Aijalon"* that the *"sun stood still, and the moon stopped"*? (Joshua 10:12-13).

You can alter the plans of the devil against you by opening your mouth and declaring what you want to see as an outcome according to God's Word. That is why the Lord says in **Psalm 81:10**, *"Open your mouth wide and I will fill it."* Why not boldly confess with your mouth that no weapons or agenda of the spiritual tyrants against your life shall come to pass.

Scriptural declarations are so powerful as to break the shackles of the tyrant spirits and release the blessings of God on you. Like Jesus declaring that no one shall eat of the fig tree and the tree withered, have you declared with your mouth that the cancer-like situation in your life must wither? You must take the Word of God and make it your own confession against the enemy. Act according to God's Word and you will harvest victory!

Keep confessing God's Word. Confess what God's Word says about the battle confronting you. You'll be amazed at what happens to your life as you tap into the transformational power of speaking God's Word over your life. When we confess the Word of God, we are actually confessing the Truth— and the Truth is the Word of God, not the situation that the devil brings against you. More so, we are sanctified when we confess the Word—*"Sanctify them in the Truth; Your Word is Truth"* (John 17:17).

We are to confess the Truth, not the fact. A fact is a thing that is known or proved to be true, but that may not be really the truth. I remember when I was studying basic Chemistry in high school. We learned Dalton's Atomic Theory: it was a highly-reputed undeniable theoretical fact among the scientific community but the discovery of mass spectrometry also revealed undeniable weaknesses in the Theory, leading to a modified theory called Modified Dalton's Atomic Theory.

You see, the fact is not always the truth! Always be in the knowing that the devil packages his lies as facts in the bid to lure you into accepting them as the truth. The blood-stained cloth presented to Jacob by his children as evidence that Joseph was killed by a wild animal was a fact (a piece of information used as an evidence) but not the truth. An indisputable fact is not always the true reality!

Don't allow the devil to talk you out of your miracles. You might be one confession away from your victory. Keep confessing what you want to see in your life. Don't go by what the devil says; rather, go by what God's Word says— and then, by your confessions, the truth shall usurp every lie of the devil regarding your life. Don't forget that the only way to combat the lies of the devil against you is by throwing the Truth at him. He can't stand the unwavering, unchanging, and unfailing Truth of what God's Word says about you!

We must be armed with the Truth of God's Word to recognize the lies as they come from the father of lies **(John 8:44)**. The devil has an arsenal of lies and he wields them relentlessly. With his lies, he puts the truth on trial. He put the Truth on trial when Pilate summoned Jesus and asked Him, *"What is truth?"*? **(John 18:38)**. If Jesus, Who Himself is Truth (John 14:6), would be put on trial, then it stands to reason that the truth of what God says about you will be put on trial. Your testimony will be put on trial, my dear! Has it ever occurred to you that your testimony is on trial?

Always confess the Word with your mouth! For instance, you may confess healing saying *"By His stripes [I am] healed"* **(Isaiah 53:5, NKJV)**! The sickness is a fact but the truth about the situation lies in what God says about it. Believing God for healing and confessing it can save you! Declare your confessions every day before you get into the day. Don't relent to speak it out.

Don't forget: Use your declarations and the confessions of your mouth to fight all that the enemy has registered against your life. Find the Scriptures that apply to your situation and then declare them.

LET US PRAY!

1. Reflect on how this reflection on *"Our Confessions and Declarations"* ministers to you.

2. Pray and ask God for the forgiveness of your sins using **Psalm 51.**

3. Put on the full armor of God using *"The Warrior's Prayer"* (see page 16).

4. Pray *"The Act of Spiritual Communion"* prayer (see page 17).

5. Pray **Psalm 27** (a psalm for exuberant declaration of faith).

6. **Job 22:28** says, *"You will also declare a thing, and it will be established for you"* **(NKJV).** Now standing on **Job 22:28,** begin to make the following declarations. I declare, in the name of Jesus Christ, that:
   a. I have all the grace I need today to live a victorious life:
      i. I walk in dominion;
      ii. I shall not stumble into the hands of the enemies;
      iii. I am special and extraordinary with incredible abilities;
      iv. I have wisdom far beyond my age;
      v. I may have been defeated before but from today:
         ▪ I am a victor and not a victim anymore;
         ▪ Everything I touch shall prosper and succeed;
         ▪ My going out and coming in are blessed;
         ▪ God's supernatural favor is over my life;
         ▪ I am an overcomer.
   b. I am calm and peaceful, no matter the trials:
      i. I am too blessed to be depressed;
      ii. I am too blessed to be stressed;
      iii. I am too glad to be sad;
      iv. I am too anointed to be disappointed;
      v. I am too cheerful to be fearful!

c. I am experiencing great victories, supernatural turnarounds, and miraculous breakthroughs in the midst of great impossibilities:
   i. When I speak to the "mountains", they are removed!
   ii. I may experience some setbacks now but I am making a comeback soon;
   iii. I reject having the attitude of a victim;
   iv. I will make lemonades out of life's lemons (please note: lemons suggest sourness or difficulty in life; making lemonade is turning them into something positive or desirable).

d. I am a blessing to my generation:
   i. I am the solution to the problems of my generation;
   ii. I add great values to other's lives;
   iii. I will store up blessings for my future generations;
   iv. I will meet people who are willing to go out of their way to help me achieve my dreams.

e. God's incredible blessings are all over my life;

f. I will always experience God's faithfulness;

g. It is not too late to accomplish everything God has placed in my heart;

h. I have a legacy of faith over my life;

i. I am grateful for who God is in my life and for what He's done and still doing, and continue to do;

j. God will accelerate His plan for my life as I put my trust in Him;

k. Unexpected blessings are coming my way;

l. God has a great plan for my life;

m. God will do exceedingly abundantly above all that I ask or think;

n. God is bringing about new seasons of growth in my life;

o. I will use the words of my mouth to bless people;

p. I have a sound mind filled with good thoughts, not thoughts of defeat;

q. There is an anointing of ease (not dis-ease) upon my life;

    r. I will make it in life. I will be one of the people who beats the odds;

    s. *"I shall not die, but I shall live, and recount the deeds of the Lord"* (Psalm 118:17);

    t. God is working all things together for my good;

    u. *"With joy, [I shall] draw water from the wells of salvation"* (Isaiah 12:3);

    v. *"No weapon that is fashioned against [me] shall prosper"* (Isaiah 54:17);

    w. *"My mouth will declare [God's] praise"* (Psalm 51:15);

    x. I am the righteousness of God in Christ Jesus;

    y. God is pleased with me. He is on my side;

    z. I declare an open heaven over my life;

7. Go on making declarations and confessions over your life as the Holy Spirit leads *(at least 5mins)*.

8. Thank the Lord Jesus Christ and cover this prayer with His Most Precious Blood (7 times).

DAY 9 - Part II: Warfare Prayers

Note:

- God promises that His Word never returns void (**Isaiah 55:11**). When, by the declarations and the confessions of your mouth, you apply the Word of God to your life and your specific needs, you will experience the power of God's Word. God listens to the declarations and the confessions of your mouth. So, mean it when you declare them! God assures you: *"I will do to you the very things I heard you say"* (**Numbers 14:28**).

- The enemy wants to hold you to condemnation by the very word you have spoken. Don't speak words of condemnation unto your life. Speak the Word of God over your life!

- **Assignment:** Look at yourself in the mirror and begin to bless yourself. Speak into yourself the very words you want to see take shape in your life!

1. Offer songs to the Lord.

2. Use **Psalm 51** to ask God for the forgiveness of your sins. Begin to make the following declarations of renunciation:
   a. I renounce and uproot out of my heart hatred, anger, resentment, lack of forgiveness, bitterness, and envy. Come out of me now, in the name of Jesus Christ;
   b. I renounce fear, doubt, unbelief, and every tormenting spirit. Come out of me now, in the name of Jesus Christ;
   c. I renounce any ungodly generational covenants that my ancestors have made going back ten generations. Let them be broken now, in the name of Jesus Christ;
   d. I renounce any allegiances to the kingdom of darkness knowingly or unknowingly, in the name of Jesus Christ;
   e. I renounce every word of negative confession I have spoken that gives the devil legal rights over my life. Let them be broken now, in the name of Jesus Christ;
   f. I renounce every false word of prophecy spoken over my destiny, my family, my marriage, my children, and my ministry, in the name of Jesus Christ.

3. Put on the full armor of God using *"The Warrior's Prayer"* (see page 16).

4. Pray *"The Act of Spiritual Communion"* prayer (see page 17).

5. The good things that are at the point of death in my life, receive life now, in the name of Jesus Christ.

6. My mornings will be good, my afternoons will be better, my evenings will be glorious, and my nights will be peaceful, in Jesus the name of Jesus Christ.

7. O Lord Jesus Christ, let the words of my mouth and the meditations of my heart be acceptable in Your sight (Psalm 19:14)—in the name of Jesus Christ.

8. O Lord Jesus Christ, set a watch over my mouth and keep the door of my lips. Let not evil communication proceed from my lips, in the name of Jesus Christ.

9. Lord Jesus Christ, help me to please You in what I think, say, and do, in the name of Jesus Christ.

10. I break off any backlash, any retaliation, or any transfer of spirits that is trying to come against me, my family, my loved ones and my finances, in the name of Jesus Christ.

11. In the name of Jesus Christ, I declare that Satan has no power over me. I have been delivered from the power of darkness, and translated into the Kingdom of God's dear Son **(Colossians 1:13)**.

12. Begin to make intercessory prayers of declarations (pray in the name of Jesus Christ).
    a. I decree and declare that our societies and communities are free from ..... (*pick from the following list*), in the name of Jesus Christ.

    - Violence
    - Unemployment
    - Illiteracy
    - Poverty
    - Homelessness
    - Rape
    - Domestic violence
    - Lawlessness
    - Incest
    - Terrorism
    - Drug-abuse
    - Alcoholism
    - Perversion
    - Secularization
    - Witchcraft
    - Cultic activities
    - Satanic technologies
    - Bewitchment
    - Famine
    - Economic hardship
    - Incurable diseases
    - Abortion
    - Ethnic cleansing
    - Indifferences

b. I decree and declare that our families are free from ..... (*pick from the following list*), in the name of Jesus Christ.

- Domestic Violence
- Incest
- Dysfunction
- Hunger
- Lack
- Lying
- Shame
- Child-abuse
- Neglect & abandonment

c. I decree and declare that our marriages are free from ..... (*pick from the following list*), in the name of Jesus Christ.

- Cheating
- Adultery
- Spousal abuse
- Divorce
- Emotional trauma
- Abandonment

d. I decree and declare that our businesses are free from ..... (*pick from the following list*), in the name of Jesus Christ.

- Crime
- Bankruptcy
- Loss of clients

e. I decree and declare that our schools are free from ..... (*pick from the following list*), in the name of Jesus Christ.

- Ignorance
- Perversion
- Drugs
- Rebellion
- Secularism
- Discrimination
- Gang-life
- Illiteracy

f. I decree and declare that our Churches are free from ..... (*pick from the following list*), in the name of Jesus Christ.

- Compromise
- Carnality
- Luke-warmness
- Worldliness
- Disunity
- Denominationalism
- Immorality

g. I decree and declare that our Governments are free from ..... (*pick from the following list*), in the name of Jesus Christ.

- Tyranny
- Dictatorship
- Coup d'état
- Greed
- Dishonesty
- Thievery
- Cruelty
- Harshness
- Severity
- Insensitivity
- Bigotry
- Bias

13. I shall prosper in all things and be in good health, just as my soul prospers (3 John 1:2), in the name of Jesus Christ.

14. My gates shall receive the wealth of nations, in the name of Jesus Christ.

15. I shall not experience ruin and destruction, in the name of Jesus Christ.

16. The season of sadness and depression in my life shall be replaced with the joy of the Lord, in the name of Jesus Christ.

17. The season of lack in my life shall be replaced with abundance, in the name of Jesus Christ.

18. The favor of the Lord shall encompass me like the waters of the sea, in the name of Jesus Christ.

19. My children shall grow to be great world leaders, innovators, trailblazers, standard bearer of ..... (*pick from the following list*), in the name of Jesus Christ.
    - Excellence
    - Honesty
    - Morality
    - Integrity
    - Credibility
    - Righteousness

20. Go on making declarations and confession over your life as led by the Holy Spirit (*at least 5mins*).
    a. Prophesy unto your life the opposite of the problems confronting your life (declaring each one in the name of Jesus Christ).
    b. Prophesy unto your children, family members, career, prayer life, and so on!

21. Begin to thank the Lord Jesus Christ now:
    a. Lord Jesus, I thank You for endorsing the declarations and the confessions of my mouth;
    b. Thank You, Lord Jesus, for teaching me how to use my

declarations and the confessions of my mouth to live victoriously.

22. I cover this prayer with the Most Precious Blood of Jesus Christ (7 times).

Chapter 4

Our Testimony

"They overcame him by the Blood of the Lamb and by the word of their testimony, and they loved not their lives unto the death"
(Revelation 12:11).

[Other suggested Bible passages to read:
1 Samuel 17:34-36, 2 Samuel 5:17, Acts 22:1-21,
Acts 24:10-21, Acts 26: 1-27, Acts 4: 14-16].

DAY 8 - Part I: Reflection

Skeptics may refute something you believe. They may even question the Bible or the existence of God. However, this doesn't negate the power of God's Word; rather, it confirms for us that we're living in an age that refutes the testimony of Jesus Christ **(Revelation 19:10)**. Something that cannot be refuted, however, is the first-hand testimony that we carry with us. This is why first-hand testimony is allowed in a court of law!

God has a track record of proven testimonies of victories for His people who seek His help. Some time ago, God gave David a testimony when the lion came to take his father's lamb. He confronted the lion and God helped him kill the lion, saving the life of the lamb (1 Samuel 17:34-35). In another occasion, a bear came to snatch a lamb from the flock. God also helped David kill it, and the life of the lamb was saved. In these two events, the lion would have killed David, but God gave him great testimonies as he was not only delivered, but he was also able to snatch the lamb from the lion's mouth and then killed the lion. David killed the killer. These were powerful testimonies in the life of David!

King Saul didn't know about the testimony of David. So, when he heard that David wanted to confront Goliath, the King wanted to talk him out of it, saying, *"You are not able to go against this Philistine to fight with him; for you are just a boy, and he has been a warrior from his youth"* (1 Samuel 17:33). David knew that the same God who gave him testimony over the lion and bear would also give him another testimony over Goliath.

Therefore, armed with this testimony, he went forth to confront another killer—Goliath, the champion of the Philistines. Choosing not to wear the armor King Saul gave to him, David, rather, wore the armor of his testimony into the battlefield. Listen to David sharing his testimony with King Saul:

> *"But David said to Saul, 'Your servant used to keep sheep for his father; and whenever a lion or a bear came and took a lamb from the flock, I went after it and struck it down, rescuing the lamb from its mouth; and if it turned against me, I would catch it by the jaw, strike it down, and kill it. Your servant has killed both lions and bears; and this uncircumcised Philistine shall be like one of them since he has defied the armies of the living God'"*
> **(1 Samuel 17:34-36).**

His testimony assured him that God was going to fight for Him again. When you carry your God-given testimony of yesterday, you can, with confidence, get into the battlefields of today to carry your victory. David remembered the faithfulness of God in the past and believed Him for another testimony. Surely, testimony begets testimonies! Testifying to what God did for you attracts more testimonies to your life.

While it is important in the battles that you go through in life to be strengthened by the victory stories that God gave to other people, it's more important to look back and see the victories that God has given to you personally. That personal testimony is a great force to propel you into the next battle.

The enemy may come at you with lies and deception, but he cannot convince you that what God has done for you didn't really happen. It's your personal testimony, and it has great power! It is the final word to assure you that the God who gave you the testimony of yesterday shall prove Himself again to deliver you. However, while the enemy can't refute your testimony, he can cause you to forget your testimony—knowing that if you use your testimony, you will be victorious again. He knows that with your testimony, you will have the power to stand in faith that God will come through for you again! The enemy himself knows the power of testimony. He knows that it is a powerful weapon in your arsenal. Do you wonder why most times, people get attacked when they get or give testimony? Was it not when the Philistines heard the testimony of David—that he had been anointed King over Israel—that they came after him? (**2 Samuel 5:17**). The overcoming power of personal testimony continually attracts the attention of the enemy.

We know that our testimony is a weapon because by it (and the Blood of the Lamb), the enemy was defeated—*"They overcame [the enemy] by the blood of the Lamb and by the word of their testimony"* (**Revelation 12:11**). Our testimony assaults satanic strongholds with overwhelming force. In fact, it is God's atomic spiritual bomb against the enemy!

Regrettably, our personal testimony is a weapon of tremendous power that is so often neglected. Believers ought to use to full effect this unusual weapon always. We cannot afford silence in the matter of our own testimony. It is appropriate not only to recount the personal testimonies that God gave to us, but also to share them. When Jesus delivered the Gerasene Demoniac from bondage, He told him to go and share his personal testimony with his people— *"Go home to your friends, and tell them how much the Lord has done for you, and what mercy he has shown you"* (Mark 5:19).

On this note, the Psalmist declares: *"Come and hear, all you who fear God, and I will tell what He has done for me"* (Psalm 66:16). Apostle Paul frequently gave his testimony of an encounter with the Lord Jesus (Acts 22:1-21, Acts 26: 1-27). In his letter to Timothy, Paul wrote saying: *"Do not be ashamed, then, of the testimony about our Lord"* (2 Timothy 1:8).

The first century Church thrived on the power of their testimonies:

1. The man who was born blind, but later affirmed *"now I see,"* was incontrovertible proof of the Power of Christ (John 9:25).

2. The lame man at the gate of the temple was healed and walking around. The opposers of the Apostles said, *"We cannot deny it"* (Acts 4: 14-16).

Don't allow the enemy to take your eyes off the shelf of your testimonies. The enemy knows very well that if he can get you to focus on the negative things, or on what you *don't* have, or on the bad things going on in your life right now, he can make you forget all the testimonies of good things that God has done for you in the past. Many have lost the fight this way!

Don't forget the ways God has come through for you. Don't forget all the miracles God has done in your life. Don't forget all the ways God has provided for you when you had nothing. Don't forget the healing that God has done for you. There are your testimonies! There are your ingredients for the next war! Like David, wear the cloak of your testimony to the battlefield!

Before concluding this chapter, it is important to let us know that testimony is not only the things that we say. The way we live our life is also a testimony to unbelievers as well! **Philippians 1:27** encourages us: *"Live your life in a manner worthy of the Gospel of Christ."*

LET US PRAY!

1. Reflect on how this reflection on *"Our Testimony"* ministers to you.

2. Pray and ask God for the forgiveness of your sins using **Psalm 51.**

3. Put on the full armor of God using *"The Warrior's Prayer"* (see page 16).

4. Pray *"The Act of Spiritual Communion"* prayer (see page 17).

5. Pray **Psalm 145** (pay attention to verse 7 saying, *"They will give a testimony of your great goodness and will joyfully sing of your righteousness"*).

6. I overcome the enemy by the Blood of the Lamb and by the word of my testimony **(Revelation 12:11).**

7. I am coming out with all my testimonies, in the name of Jesus Christ.

8. In the name of Jesus Christ, I shift into a position of dominion and authority, like David. After killing "the lion and the bear," I shall also kill every "lion", "bear" or "Goliath" in my life, in the name of Jesus Christ.

9. The testimony of the Bible is that when the children of Israel cried out to You, You delivered them. O Lord, if You do not

intervene in this situation (*mention them*), there will be no way out of it. Therefore, Lord Jesus Christ, I cry out to You today:

    a. Let all my buried testimonies come out of the graves;

    b. Let all my embalmed testimonies come out of the walls;

    c. Let all my dry and dead testimonies come back to life;

    d. Let all my delayed testimonies be released to me;

    e. Let all my arrested testimonies come forth;

    f. Let all my miscarried testimonies be restored;

    g. Let all the devourers of my testimonies be destroyed;

    h. Let all the contentions over my testimonies be arrested and silenced.

10. Every embargo placed on my testimony must be lifted, in the name of Jesus Christ.

11. Thank the Lord Jesus Christ and cover this prayer with His Most Precious Blood (7 times).

DAY 9 - Part II: Warfare Prayers

Note:

- Your personal testimony is one of the most devastating weapons against Satan. The devil hates your testimony. There is victory embedded in your testimony. Use it!

- Pope Saint Paul VI said: *"Contemporary man needs testimony more than arguments."*

1. Sing songs to the Lord Jesus Christ, recounting His goodness to you.

2. Pray and ask God for the forgiveness of your sins.

    a. Examination of Conscience (*if guilty of any of the following, ask God for mercy and forgiveness*):

     i. Have I fabricated or exaggerated a testimony?

    ii. Do I brag or glorify myself in presenting my testimony?

   iii. Do I refuse to share the testimonies of what God did for me?

   iv. Do I doubt the testimony of what God did when I hear them?

  b. Pray **Psalm 51** to ask God for the forgiveness of your sins.

3. Put on the full armor of God using *"The Warrior's Prayer"* (see page 16).

4. Pray *"The Act of Spiritual Communion"* prayer (see page 17).

5. Lord Jesus, grant that my life gives true witness of Your love and testimony of Your deliverance. Make me a symbol of good news for others, in the name of Jesus Christ.

6. Lord God, as You put the testimony of hedge of protection on Job's family, so I ask You to keep the same hedge of protection around my family, my mind, my heart, my emotions, my ministry, and my relationship with You.
   a. Encamp Your powerful Angels to surround us every day;
   b. Surround us with a supernatural wall of fire;
   c. Send a host of ministering angels to attend to our hurts, our needs, our pain, and our infirmities;
   d. Protect us from every assault of the evil one.

7. Let the venomous spirits causing toxic relationships in my life and family be arrested, in the name of Jesus Christ.

8. I decree and declare that no more shall I miscarry my testimonies, in the name of Jesus Christ.

9. In the name of Jesus Christ, I intercept the activities of all demonic spirits targeting my testimonies. In the name of

Jesus Christ, I come against...
a. All spiritual night hunters;
b. All blood-sucking spirits (vampires), marine spirits, spirits of the deep and underworld, and all forms of animal spirits (e.g. snake spirits, vulture, and owl spirits);
c. I decree and declare that they are exposed.

10. I decree that all evil inquiries, fault-finding missions, astral-projections, and observations of satanic surveyors on a mission to bring down my testimonies must fail, in the name of Jesus Christ.

11. I stand on my past testimonies to declare new testimonies in my life, in the name of Jesus Christ. Begin to pray in the name of Jesus Christ:
a. I command everything that the enemy has swallowed up to be released to me right now. I command my..... (*pick from the following list*) to be released to me in the name of Jesus Christ;

- Children
- Marriage
- Family
- Money
- Business
- Opportunities
- Destiny
- Success
- Miracles
- Breakthroughs

b. I have new testimonies, and they cannot be taken away from me. Therefore, in the name of Jesus Christ:
   i. I have divine insights and revelations;
   ii. I have creative ideas and inventions;
   iii. I have cutting-edge strategies and tactics.
c. Those who have constructed satanic snares and traps against me, let their plans be voided and their assignments frustrated, in the name of Jesus Christ;
d. Let God paralyze whatever hinders me from moving into greatness in life:

    i. Roll away the obstacles blocking my breakthroughs;

    ii. Overthrow satanic tables of negotiations;

    iii. Destroy every evil device fashioned for my failure.

12. *"I am praying not only for these disciples but also for all who will ever believe in me because of their testimony"* (John 17:20, NLT). Therefore, Lord Jesus (*pray in the name of Jesus Christ*):

    a. Let my testimony bring glory to Your Mighty Name;

    b. Let my testimony be the key to unlock someone else's prison.

13. Lord Jesus Christ, give me a single testimony that will silence those mocking me, in the name of Jesus Christ. Continue to pray the following in the name of Jesus Christ:

    a. Lord Jesus, please, give me the testimony that will:

        i. Turn every mess in my life into a message;

        ii. Turn every test in my life into a testimony;

        iii. Turn every trial into a triumph.

    b. Let my testimony, let my testimony take me from being a victim to becoming a victor.

14. Begin to thank the Lord Jesus Christ now:

    a. Lord Jesus, I thank You for the testimonies You have given to me;

    b. Thank You, Lord Jesus, for teaching me how to use my personal testimonies to live victoriously.

15. I cover this prayer with the Most Precious Blood of Jesus Christ (7 times).

Chapter 5

Praying in Tongues

"For if I pray in a tongue, my spirit prays but my mind is unproductive"

(1 Corinthians 14:14)

[Other suggested Bible passages to read:
(1 Corinthians 14:4-17, Ephesians 6:18, Mark 16:17,
1 Corinthians 12:8-11, Jude 20].

DAY 10 - Part I: Reflection

Praying in tongues is a powerful offensive weapon that we can use to wage spiritual warfare against the unseen enemies. It is an armor of God and a key part of our weaponry. It carries a hidden power necessary for interrupting the enemy's agenda.

Our tongue is like a sharp razor, a sword or even a knife —**Psalm 52:2** says, *"Your tongue is like a sharp razor"* and **Psalm 57:4** says that *"Their tongues [are] sharp swords."* What do you do with a sword or a knife when an enemy is all out to kill you? You fight the enemy with it, don't you? You can even, with it, kill the enemy. Rightly, *"Death and life are in the power of the tongue"* (Proverbs 18:21). Prayer warlords must, therefore, *"sharpen their tongues like swords"* (Psalm 64:3, GNT).

Similarly, our tongue is like an arrow— *"Their tongue is a deadly arrow"* (Jeremiah 9:8). Our tongue is also like a bow that is used to shoot arrows—Jeremiah 9:3 says, *"They bend their tongues like bows."* In order for a bow to launch a projectile against an enemy, it is required to have some power and strength in it. Just as the Lord says in **Proverbs 18:21**, there is power in the tongue.

Now that you know how powerful tongues are, would you not agree with me that a warring child of God who knows how to use his tongue in spiritual battles actually has an upgraded weapon? Such child of God becomes even more deadly to the enemy because his tongue becomes like *"a bronze arrow [that] will strike them through"* (Job 20:24).

You must desire to upgrade your tongue to become like a bronze arrow that strikes and pierces through the enemy. A tongue that is not upgraded is like a wooden arrow or a straw. It is not fit for spiritual battles. Would you not pity a man going to fight an enemy that wants to kill him with a straw? You know he is already defeated! A bow made out of bronze or steel is more powerful than the one that is made from wood or straw.

Be it known to you that every time you pray in tongues, the Holy Spirit strengthens your inner man, and unmasks the enemy. When in the heat of spiritual combat, it is easy for us to become weary in the place of prayer, often not knowing what or how to pray.

Through praying in tongues, *"The Spirit Himself makes intercession for us"* (Romans 8:26). It causes us to line up our spirit with the Holy Spirit (Romans 8:16-17). When we pray in tongues, we are responding to the prompt of the Spirit to release the power to intercept every evil that is either going on or about to go on in the spirit. It quickens to be brought into light demons that are hiding.

What a wonderful weapon of deliverance for routing demonic forces. Praying in tongues is a demon chaser! This weapon is simply amazing. Use it!

LET US PRAY!

1. Reflect on how this reflection on *"Praying in Tongues"* ministers to you.

2. Pray and ask God for the forgiveness of your sins using **Psalm 51.**

3. Put on the full armor of God using *"The Warrior's Prayer"* (see page 16).

4. Pray *"The Act of Spiritual Communion"* prayer (see page 17).

5. Pray **Psalm 110** (psalm for the assurance of victory)

6. Thank You, Lord Jesus, for giving me a tongue that speaks healing and life, in the name of Jesus Christ.

7. Lord Jesus, divide the tongues of the enemies and bring their plans to naught, in the name of Jesus Christ.

8. In the name of Jesus Christ, I release the tongue of prophecy to the four winds of heaven **(Daniel 7:2):**
   a. That my blessings that have died prematurely and dried up (because of satanic activities) be quickened back to life;
   b. That every blessing meant for my life come together (my health/my family/my prayer life/my business/... is coming together);
   c. That the cause of Christ is advancing in every region of the world;
   d. That every evil attachment to my life is broken;
   e. That I arise in the spirit of Zerubbabel to question: *"What are you, O Great Mountain? (Zechariah 4:7a).*

Then I decree: *"Before Zerubbabel, you [mountain] shall become a plain"* (Zechariah 4:7b). Hallelujah!

   f. That my spirit shall not be held hostage or besieged;

   g. That I break free from the snare of the fowler.

9. Ask the Holy Spirit to lead you into praying in tongues according to the will of God.

10. Thank the Lord Jesus Christ and cover this prayer with His Most Precious Blood (7 times).

DAY 11 - Part II: Warfare Prayers

Note:

- God has provided us with praying in tongues as a weapon for spiritual warfare. Praying in tongues enables us to have spirit-to-Spirit communication with God. It charges our spirits like a battery charger powers a battery.

- This weapon throws the devil into confusion as he does not understand what you are speaking and, at the same time, he sees piercing flaming arrows flying towards him. I encourage you to keep this weapon in your arsenal and use it along with all your other weapons.

- If you have this gift, use it in this prayer. If you don't have, ask for it. Sing songs to the Lord.

1. Use **Psalm 51** to ask God for the forgiveness of your sins.

2. Put on the full armor of God using *"The Warrior's Prayer* (see page 16).

3. Pray *"The Act of Spiritual Communion"* prayer (see page 17).

4. In the name of Jesus Christ, as I begin to pray (praying in tongues, if led by the Holy Spirit):

a. Let this prayer cause terror to strike the agents of darkness sent to attack me or anything connected to my life with thunders, lightning, and hailstones;

b. Let this prayer cause coals of fire to fall upon the agents of darkness:

   i. Let their poisonous fang-like weapons become ineffective;

   ii. Let fire burn their covens, altars, and temples.

c. Let this prayer resist territorial strongholds;

d. Let this prayer split open the gates of psychological prisons and demonic entanglements;

e. Let this prayer deliver us from stigmatization, emotional blackmail, satanic limitations and restrictions, satanic illusions, addictions, cultural entrenchments, cultic strongholds, bewitchments, and ungodly traditions.

f. Let this prayer cause us to wear a cloak of favor;

g. Let this prayer cause me to disengage demonic firing triggers;

h. Let this prayer make me irresponsive to satanic projections;

i. Let this prayer cause the works of the devil to be destroyed over my body, over my family, over my loved ones, over the Church, over the Government, over my neighborhood, and over the entire nation.

8. In the name of Jesus Christ, I command every satanic agent assigned to hold up or slow down my blessings to be frustrated, foiled, and hindered from fulfilling their assignment.

9. Let every prophetic word spoken upon my life be manifested in its proper time and season, in the name of Jesus Christ!

10. Lord Jesus Christ, I ask in Your Precious Name that I may never speak any cruel word which is not true:

a. Or being true, is not the whole truth;

b. Or being wholly truth but merciless.

11. Ask the Holy Spirit to lead you into praying in tongues according to the will of God.

12. Begin to thank the Lord Jesus Christ:
    a. I thank You, Lord Jesus, for teaching me how praying in tongues can be used to fight a spiritual war;
    b. I thank You, Lord Jesus, for turning things around in my favor in the course of this prayer.

13. I cover this prayer with the Most Precious Blood of Jesus Christ (7 times).

Chapter 6

Praying with the Elements

"Truly I tell you, if you say to this mountain, 'Be taken up and thrown into the sea,' and if you do not doubt in your heart, but believe that what you say will come to pass, it will be done for you."

(Mark 11:23)

[Other suggested Bible passages to read:
Haggai 2:6-9, Genesis 19:12-29, Joshua 10:12-13, I Kings 18:16-45, Exodus 7:8-13, Exodus 8- Exodus 12].

DAY 12 - Part I: Reflection

God has lots of powerful weapons in His armory that would be released to engage the enemy as we pray. All things created by God can be used as weapons in spiritual battles. Using created things or elements in prayer as a weapon of prayer can cause a deadly blow or havoc to the kingdom of darkness in the scale that the enemy has not experienced before. For instance, fire and brimstone are a created thing—and these were what God used to destroy the people of Sodom and Gomorrah **(Genesis 19:24)**. The Red Sea is a created thing, and this was what God used as a powerful weapon to destroy the Egyptian armies when they were chasing the people of Israel.

Rain and water are created things: God used them to destroy the wicked generation in Noah's time. On this note, a warring child of God might choose to make a prayer calling liquid fire or red-hot brimstones from heaven to destroy all the witchcraft covens or occult altars 100-miles radius from where he is praying.

You might pray to God to release torrents of concentrated sulphuric acid to fall like rain and flood every dominion of darkness. [Even a mist of sulphuric acid in the air can kill, not to talk of a flood of its concentrated form!] I told you earlier that the use of elements can potentially cause an unprecedented deadly blow on the enemy.

Supersize your weapons of warfare!

Jesus tells us in **Mark 11:23** saying, *"Truly I tell you, if you say to this mountain, 'Be taken up and thrown into the sea,' and if you do not doubt in your heart, but believe that what you say will come to pass, it will be done for you."* You might choose to command the mountain to be taken up and bury alive the gathering of the dominion of darkness. You might also, with faith, command the mountain to move and block the enemy's airways, highways, waterways, tunnels, and subways. Have you thought of commanding rocks to fly with laser-speed as stones of fire to kill every Goliath sitting on your blessings?

Joshua prayed to God saying, *"Sun, stand still at Gibeon, and Moon, in the valley of Aijalon"* (**Joshua 10:12**). The result of that prayer was that *"The sun stood still, and the moon stopped until the nation took vengeance on their enemies"* (**Joshua 10:13**). Moses spoke to the earth to open and swallow up the clan of Korah, Dathan, and Abiram— and *"The earth opened its mouth and swallowed them up, along with their **households**—everyone who belonged to Korah and all their goods"* (**Numbers 16:32**). Elijah commanded the sky never to release *"dew nor rain"* except by his word (**1 Kings 17:1**). It came to pass!

Jesus spoke to the wind and the sea saying, *"'Peace! Be still!' Then the wind ceased, and there was a dead calm"* (Mark 4:39). Also in another occasion, Jesus spoke to the fig tree saying, *"May no one ever eat fruit from you again"* (Mark 11:14). Mark 11:20 testifies, *"In the morning as they passed by, they saw the fig tree withered away to its roots."* Prophet Jeremiah spoke to the earth saying, *"O earth, earth, earth, Hear the word of the Lord! Thus says the Lord: 'Write this man down as childless, a man who shall not prosper in his days; for none of his descendants shall prosper'"* (Jeremiah 22:29-30, NKJV).

Do you notice that the sun and the moon listened to Joshua? The wind, the sea, and the tree listened to Jesus? The earth listened to Moses and also to Prophet Jeremiah? Likewise, you can pray and command the sun, moon, stars, planets, constellations, earth, air, wind, fire, water, light, darkness, storm, rain, time, deserts, mountains, trees, tomorrow, today, morning, afternoon, evening, night, or any other matter to obey you. These listed items are called elements.

I have an irrefutable case to make here: You can command the elements like Joshua, Moses or our Lord Jesus with faith and they will obey you because of the power of God confirming your declarations that are in line with the mind of God. Therefore, you can command the elements against the diabolical operations of the tyrant spirits.

Aaron's staff (an element) was a weapon to swallow all the poisonous snakes of Pharaoh's magicians and sorcerers (**Exodus 7:8-13**). Moses used this warfare tactic against the Egyptians as described in **Exodus 10:22-23**—*"So Moses stretched out his hand toward heaven, and there was dense darkness in all the land of Egypt for three days. People could not see one another, and for three days they could not move from where they were, but all the Israelites had light where they lived."* As we can see, Moses used the elements to hold the Egyptians hostage for three days. You can use the elements to keep spiritual enemies under a spiritual "house arrest". Yes, you can!

The ten plagues of Egypt were occasions of God using the elements as weapon of warfare against Egypt **(Exodus 7- Exodus 12)**. These plagues or elements are:

1. The first plague: Water is changed into blood **(Exodus 7:14– 24)**

2. The second plague: The plague of frogs **(Exodus 7:25–8:15)**

3. The third plague: The plague of lice **(Exodus 8:16-19)**

4. The fourth plague: The plague of flies **(Exodus 8:20-32)**

5. The fifth plague: The plague of livestock **(Exodus 9:1–7)**

6. The sixth plague: The plague of boils **(Exodus 9:8–12)**

7. The seventh plague: The plague of hail and fire **(Exodus 9:13–35)**

8. The eighth plague: The plague of locusts **(Exodus 10:1–20)**

9. The ninth plague: The plague of darkness **(Exodus 10:21–29)**

10. The tenth plague: The plague of death of firstborn **(Exodus 11:1–12:36)**

My dear child of God, the power of praying with the elements is great. I hope you can't wait to use the power of the elements to hold hostage every spiritual tyrant attacking you. You may consider using your prayers to hold them hostage up till the second coming of our Lord Jesus Christ.

LET US PRAY!

1. Reflect on how this reflection on *"Praying with the Elements"* ministers to you.

2. Pray and ask God for the forgiveness of your sins using **Psalm 51.**

3. Put on the full armor of God using *"The Warrior's Prayer* (see page 16).

4. Pray *"The Act of Spiritual Communion"* prayer (see page 17).

5. Pray **Psalm 121** (pay attention to verse 6 in which the Lord promises that the elements shall smite you: *"The sun shall not strike you by day, nor the moon by night"* (Psalm 121:6));

6. Address the earth with authority: Take your rightful position in **Jeremiah 22:29 (KJV)** and declare, *"O earth, earth, earth, hear the word of the Lord"* *(praying in the name of Jesus Christ):*

   a. *"O earth, earth, earth,"* turn red hot against satanic establishments at work against me;

   b. *"O earth, earth, earth,"* release your volcanoes and let your molten rocks (lava) flow like a river into the territories where the devil is glorified;

   c. *"O earth, earth, earth,"* open your mouth like in the days of Moses and swallow up every dominion of evil against me and my family;

   d. *"O earth, earth, earth,"* as you opened your *"mouth and swallowed up the flood which the dragon had spewed out of his mouth"* to carry the woman away **(Revelations 12:15-16)**, so I ask you now to open your mouth and swallow up every encroaching attack against me and my family;

   e. *"O earth, earth, earth,"* as Aaron's staff swallowed up the snakes of Pharaoh's magicians **(Exodus 7:12)**, so I command the mountains of the earth to swallow up every "mountain" in my life. Therefore, Lord Jesus:

      i. Level the *"destroying mountains"* to the ground (Jeremiah 51:25a);

      ii. Leave *"destroying mountains...in [heaps of] ashes"* (Jeremiah 51:25b).

   f. *"O earth, earth, earth,"* expose every spirit hiding under you as the Fire of God causes your *"rocks [to] turn into a pool of water"* (Psalm 114:8);

g. *"O earth, earth, earth,"* let your mountains block the enemy's airways, highways, waterways, tunnels, and subways;

h. *"O earth, earth, earth,"* shake your sea, your dry lands, and all the nations, *"so that the treasure of all nations shall come"* to me (Haggai 2:6-9);

i. *"O earth, earth, earth,"* let your deserts and all uninhabitable places begin to torment all evil forces coming after me (command the spirits to march to the hot deserts of the earth);

j. *"O earth, earth, earth,"* release your earthquake to destroy every satanic altar that has been set up against me, my family, my loved ones, my ministry, and all that belong to me;

k. *"O earth, earth, earth,"* release all my blessings (and those of my loved ones) buried inside you for ages.

7. Address the seas with authority: Take your rightful position in **Isaiah 19:5** and declare, *"The waters of the Nile will be dried up"* (*praying in the name of Jesus Christ*):

a. You "Sea" of affliction flowing into my life, dry up right now!

b. You "Sea," as in the days of Pharaoh, drown every "Pharaoh" chasing my destiny;

c. You "Sea," boil! Begin to cook the marine spirits as I pray!

d. You "Sea," you shall not be a channel to transport an evil load into my life;

e. You "Sea," become a burning sulfur! Overflow exceedingly as in the days of Noah, destroying all satanic commonwealths!

f. O you----- (*pick from the following list*) cooperate with me in this prayer by turning as a weapon against every force coming against me, in the name of Jesus Christ.

- Air
- Water
- Sun
- Moon
- Star
- Wind
- Storms
- Trees
- Mountains
- Time
- Fire
- Rain

8. Thank the Lord Jesus Christ and cover this prayer with His Most Precious Blood (7 times).

DAY 13 - Part II: Warfare Prayers

Note:

- Joshua and his men had a fierce and fearsome battle. The armies clashed all day, and Joshua's men were winning. However, as night approached with an unfinished battle, Joshua needed more daylight to finish the contest. So he did the unthinkable: Asking God to make the sun to stand still. And God did! What does it mean for you that Joshua commanded the sun to stand still and the sun stood still (**Joshua 10:12-13**)? Believe God for the impossible. Which element do you want to command for your next testimony?

1. Sing songs to the Lord.

2. Use **Psalm 51** to ask God for the forgiveness of your sins.

3. Put on the full armor of God using *"The Warrior's Prayer"* (see page 16).

4. Pray *"The Act of Spiritual Communion"* prayer (see page 17).

5. As I engage in this prayer, I decree that all the plagues that afflicted Egypt in the time of Moses are being activated a million times more to afflict all the agents of the kingdom of darkness attacking me, in the name of Jesus Christ,

6. *"As fire causes wood to burn and water to boil"* (Isaiah 64:2, NLT), so shall the fire do to the kingdom of darkness, in the name of Jesus Christ.

7. *"On the wicked, He will rain coals of fire and sulfur; a scorching wind shall be the portion of their cup"* (Psalm 11:6)

8. I command all the elemental forces of nature to refuse to co-operate with my enemies, in the name of Jesus Christ.
   a. I speak to the sun, the moon, and the stars: *"You must not smite me for the Lord says this concerning me"*: **"The sun shall not strike you by day, nor the moon by night"** (Psalm 121:6);
   b. I command every power manipulating the elements against me to be arrested, for there is no incantations or enchantments against me that shall prosper **(Numbers 23:23)**;
   c. The fire of the enemy shall not burn me;
   d. I cancel all appointments with sorrow and tragedy.

9. Let the stones of destruction, rain down upon every demonic spirit hindering my blessings, in the name of Jesus Christ.

10. I call upon heaven to release spiritual acid unto the habitation of the agents of darkness, in the name of Jesus Christ.

11. Whether I am on the sea, in the air or on the road, the evil forces there shall bow to the Christ in me, in the name of Jesus Christ.

12. I will neither be afraid of the arrow that flies by day nor the terror that comes at night **(Psalm 91:5)**, in the name of Jesus Christ.

13. Lord Jesus, show forth Your salvation in my life from day to day **(Psalm 96:2)**, in the name of Jesus Christ.

14. Begin to thank the Lord Jesus Christ for the victory granted through this prayer:
    a. Thank You, Lord Jesus Christ, for teaching me how praying with the elements can be used to fight a spiritual war;
    b. Offer songs of thanksgiving or pray **Psalm 150.**

15. I cover this prayer with the Most Precious Blood of Jesus Christ (7 times).

Chapter 7

The Authority of the Believer

"See, I have given you authority to tread on snakes and scorpions, and over all the power of the enemy; and nothing will hurt you."

(Luke 10:19)

[Other suggested Bible passages to read:
Mark 16: 17-18, Psalm 8:5-8, Genesis 1:26, Matthew 8:9-13,
Luke 9:1–2, Luke 10:17–19].

DAY 14 -Part I: Reflection

A policeman or an officer in the Armed Forces of any country is trained and equipped by the Government the officer is sworn to uphold. The officer is also given the necessary authority to discharge his/her duties. Similarly, Jesus Christ delegates His authority and power to His disciples to discharge their assigned responsibilities.

Everyone obeys the policeman not because he wears a badge, but because his badge — a sign of the authority he carries — is backed up by the full power of the Government who grants it. So too, evil spirits must obey the authority of Jesus Christ when His disciples, in pursuit of their legitimate responsibilities, administer it.

Everyone obeys the policeman or the military officer because his badge — a sign of the authority he carries — is backed up by the full power of the Government who grants it. With his authority, he can arrest, attack, or even kill in the discharge of his official duty.

In the same way, the devil and his demonic spirits must obey us because of the badge of the authority of Jesus Christ that we carry with us as His ambassadors on earth. We can, with the authority of Heaven's Government that we carry, arrest, interrupt, intercept, overthrow or destroy the agenda and operation of the kingdom of darkness. **Jeremiah 1:10** clearly ratifies this fact saying, *"See, today I appoint you over nations and over kingdoms, to pluck up and to pull down, to destroy and to overthrow, to build and to plant."* With Heaven's authority that we carry, we can, through prayers, administer legitimately the mind of Heaven (and their judicial decisions) concerning the affairs of men on earth.

Authority does not need to be sought. It is inherent in a believer or a true Christian. However, authority must be exercised to become effective. I can't imagine a policeman failing to exercise his Government-given authority during his official assignment. Such an officer is at the mercy of the enemy.

The Authority over the devil and his demonic entities comes from knowing, loving, and serving God. The authority of Heaven we carry comes from Christ, who *"called the twelve together and gave them power and authority over all demons and to cure diseases"* **(Luke 9:1)**. We don't have to be smarter or stronger than our spiritual enemy. All we need is to have Jesus Christ as the Lord of our lives. It is His authority that we are invoking.

Suppose, in a play, someone plays the role of a police officer. He wears the full police uniform and puts on his police badge. You also know that this man doesn't like you. If at the end of the play he angrily comes to you for an arrest saying, *"you are under arrest,"* would you surrender to him? I suppose the answer is *"No, I won't."* Then my question is, *"Why? Do you not see the police badge he wears?"* I am pretty sure you would say, *"Yes, I see the police badge that he bears but He does not carry the authority to arrest me."*

In the same way, the devil doesn't bother at all if we wear the badge of Christianity but do not behave like Jesus Christ. He doesn't give a hoot at all because he knows that such "Christians" don't carry the authority of Jesus that they proclaim as their Lord. In fact, unknown to such people, the devil actually uses them to carry out his own agenda! The devil can easily deal with them if he decides to. **Acts 19:11-20** tells us how the seven sons of Sceva commanded an evil spirit to depart from a possessed person, but the evil spirit questioned their authority saying, *"Jesus I know, and Paul I recognize, but who are you?"* (Acts 19:15). The situation came to a terrible climax as " *"The man in whom was the evil spirit leaped on them, mastered all of them and overpowered them so that they fled out of that house naked and wounded"* (Acts 19:16). The message is clear, isn't it?

Perhaps the least understood and among the most potent of the spiritual weapons is the believer's authority. It is an unfortunate situation when a Police officer or an Army officer does not know the authority that he carries. More unfortunate, and even more deplorable, is a child of God who does not know his or her authority in Christ. There are simply prisoners of war.

Having said this, I would go further to classify people in this world into three groups (you would have to ask yourself which group you fall into): (1) soldiers of Christ, (2) soldiers of the enemy, and (3) those who are prisoners of war. Soldiers of Christ are those who, through the authority of Jesus Christ, fight and conquer the devil and his minions. The soldiers of the enemy are the agents of darkness. They are enemies, just like the devil and his minions. The last group of people, those who are just prisoners of war, are those folks who are spiritually cold or lukewarm, and of course, inexperienced in spiritual battles. It doesn't matter whether they go by "Christians" or go to Church, as far as there is no relationship between them and Jesus Christ.

The unfortunate tragedy of our time is that so many Christians are prisoners of war. They do not know about their weapons. They do not know the authority that Christ has vested on them. They do not live the life that God designed for them. They are prisoners of war kept in cages, mistreated, and deprived by the enemy. God wants us to save them. We have to be courageous enough to push back the gates of hell as to rescue them from the powers of darkness.

In **Acts 16:16–18,** Apostle Paul and his companions met a slave girl who had a spirit of divination that brought her owners a great deal of money by fortune-telling. While she followed them for many days, Paul, very much annoyed, turned and said to the spirit, *"I command you in the name of Jesus Christ to come out of her"* (Acts 16:18, NKJV). Right there and then, the spirit came out of her at that very hour!

Paul had been discerning and praying for several days regarding the spirit in this girl, but nothing happened until when he took authority over the situation by saying, *"I command you in the name of Jesus Christ to come out of her."* There's a difference between asking God to make a demon go away, and commanding a demon to leave in the name, power, and authority of Jesus Christ. Spiritual warfare involves commands (with faith), a personal confrontation with, taking authority over, and casting evil spirits away.

In order to move with the same power as Saint Paul, it is appropriate and necessary to discern when it is appropriate to use the prayer of command or a prayer of petition. I recommend that after you have asked God for His assistance in prayer (petition), then start using the power and authority that has been given to you. The prayer with an expression of authority sounds like this, but not limited to this: *"I command you snake spirits to get out of her, in the name of Jesus Christ. I break all agreements with you, in the name of Jesus Christ."*

It is necessary to start using your God-given authority in your prayers when an evil power attacks your thoughts, health, home, ministry, environment, or workplace by commanding the evil spirit to depart in the name of Jesus Christ. This is the ultimate prayer to set up the enemy and position yourself to secure the victory you are seeking.

LET US PRAY!

1. Reflect on how this reflection on *"The Authority of the Believer"* ministers to you.

2. Pray and ask God for the forgiveness of your sins using **Psalm 51.**

3. Put on the full armor of God using *"The Warrior's Prayer"* (see page 16).

4. Pray *"The Act of Spiritual Communion"* prayer (see page 17).

5. Pray **Psalm 8** (pay attention to the authority of the believer in verse 6: *"You have given them dominion over the works of your hands; you have put all things under their feet"*).

6. I take my rightful seat of authority in Christ and I take authority over all satanic alters within a100-mile radius of this prayer. In the name of Jesus Christ, I take authority over the power of...
   a. The enemy that is responsible for building satanic altars in this region;
   b. Ancestral spirits transferring evil loads that interfere with my advancement or progress in life.

7. Devil, listen to me (you are addressing him to get his attention. Remember that you came to fight, and you are positioning yourself for your victory. You are not playing!) Therefore, in the name of Jesus Christ:

   a. I am coming against you from my position of authority;

   b. I release the thunder of God against every target that has my name on it in the enemy's camp: Be destroyed now!

   c. I release the rod of God to torment every demon that has been assigned against me;

   d. I release the plagues of Egypt on the head of every devil trying to steal my anointing, my purpose, and my destiny;

   e. I send panic into the enemy's camp:

      i. Let them attack and kill each other;

      ii. Let there be communication breakdown as I place a wall of the Most Precious Blood of Jesus Christ between them.

   f. Let the Angels of God chase down every devil and torment them until they release my blessings.

8. Thank the Lord Jesus Christ and cover this prayer with His Most Precious Blood (7 times).

DAY 15 - Part II: Warfare Prayers

Note:

- Take authority over your spiritual enemies. Specifically, exercise this authority in the name of Jesus Christ. We establish a position of authority over them, to which they must submit.

1. Sing songs to the Lord as the Holy Spirit leads.

2. Use **Psalm 51** to ask God for the forgiveness of your sins.

3. Put on the full armor of God using *"The Warrior's Prayer"* (see page 16).

4. Pray *"The Act of Spiritual Communion"* prayer (see page 17).

5. The Word of God says that I have authority to tread over serpents and scorpions. I now take authority over every strongman in my family (*name the strongman spirits, if you know them*), in the name of Jesus Christ.

6. I walk on my superior authority as a believer over the spirits operating in this region. I claim this region for Christ—in the name of Jesus Christ.

7. I take authority over issues originating from the camp of the enemy, in the name of Jesus Christ.

8. Begin to take authority over powers, abilities, and capabilities of the enemy (including their weapons of warfare). In the name of Jesus Christ:
   a. I take authority over all powers and abilities of the enemy;
   b. I disable all their weapons of warfare;
   c. I cut off every demonic strongman and I release fire against every spirit whose function is to keep me from getting to the strongman!
   d. I disable all their support and reinforcement mechanisms:
      i. Block them from assisting each other;

      ii. Let each strongman stand alone to face the fire of this prayer!

9. Exercise authority over your family members. Employ the Most Precious Blood of Jesus Christ, which has ransomed everything concerning your life, destiny, and purpose.
   a. .... (*pick from the following list*) been ransomed, in the name of Jesus Christ;

- I have
- My family has
- My future has
- My loved ones have
- My ministry has

b. My future and destiny are secured in Christ Jesus;

c. The future and destinies of my.... (*pick from the following list*) in Christ, in the name of Jesus Christ;

- Children
- Grandchildren
- God-children
- Siblings
- Ministry
- Community

d. I decree that the members my family are blessed in Christ Jesus:
   i. They shall not beg to eat;
   ii. They shall not experience homelessness or helplessness;
   iii. They shall not die prematurely.

e. I decree that the souls of all my family members are redeemed from the powers of the underworld;

f. I declare that the members of my family shall not become victims of fornication, prostitution, pornography, drugs, addictions, or gang violence;

10. Lord Jesus, thank You for purchasing redemption for me, my loved ones, and for all of mankind.

11. Begin to thank the Lord Jesus for the victory granted through this prayer:

a. Thank You Lord Jesus for teaching me how exercising my authority as a believer can be used to fight a spiritual war;

b. Offer songs of thanksgiving or pray **Psalm 149.**

12. I cover this prayer with the Most Precious Blood of Jesus Christ (7 times).

Chapter 8

Knowledge

"My people are destroyed for lack of knowledge"
(Hosea 4:6)

"In order to keep Satan from getting the upper hand over us; for we know what his plans are"
(2 Corinthians 2:11)

"Let those who boast boast in this, that they understand and know me."
(Jeremiah 9:24)

[Other suggested Bible passages to read:
1 Peter 5:8, Deuteronomy 29:29, Ephesians 6:12,
Proverbs 2:6, Daniel 2:21, Jeremiah 9:23-24, John 8:44,
2 Corinthians 4:4, 1 John 4:1, Genesis 3:1].

DAY 16 - Part I: Reflection

I once saw a kite and snake fight. The snake wanted the fight on the ground because that is its territory of power and dominance, but I watched with amazement as the kite took the fight into the air and defeated the snake. Undoubtedly, the kite had the knowledge that fighting the snake on the ground level is to fight the enemy where it is strong. The kite knew, however, that the snake is disadvantaged when the fight is taken above the ground, where it has powerful strength.

Similarly, we should have knowledge of the strengths and weaknesses of the enemy in order to defeat him. We also ought to know our own weaknesses and strengths, and fight from the position of strength. You don't fight the devil in the flesh and expect victory. He is of the flesh and, therefore, wants you to fight him in the flesh. Like the kite, we should take the enemy into God's higher grounds and fight him there! Knowledge of the enemy's capabilities is very important in spiritual warfare.

People say that knowledge is power. That also is a spiritual truth! If you would successfully fight demons out of your life, a wise step is to become knowledgeable about how the demonic world operates. Knowledge also helps you know what you are doing that opens doors for the enemy to attack you. You cannot successfully fight an enemy you don't know how he functions. In fact, you are as powerful as the amount of knowledge you have about your enemy.

On one hand, Satan gains much victories over many Christians who are not thoroughly acquainted with the spiritual arsenal God has given to them. On the other hand, we cost the devil a lot of real estate when we have good knowledge of the art of spiritual warfare. Therefore, knowledge of the spirits you fight against is one of the most powerful weapons you will have to defeat them. I would jokingly say that you can't grow more than the knowledge in your head.

God has given you powerful weapons of warfare. Every Christian in the world has a veritable arsenal of weapons at his/ her disposal. Therefore, God is not to be blamed if the devil is victorious over you because of your ignorance of spiritual battles. The Scripture says that *"My people are destroyed for lack of knowledge; because you have rejected knowledge, I reject you from being a priest to me"* (Hosea 4:6). My dear friend in Christ, what are you waiting for before you take up your key and unlock the door to God's weapon's room. This horrendous situation of walking in ignorance is shameful and must change!

I wish to take you through two things to think about. First, why does Scripture say that the devil is *"seeking whom he may devour"* (1 Peter 5:8)? The reason is that the devil cannot devour everybody! The devil can't devour people who are armed with spiritual knowledge. He won't devour you if you have knowledge of his ways and have knowledge on how to put on the whole armor of God.

The second thing I want you to think about is going to highlight how vulnerable we are when we do not have knowledge of what goes on in the spirit world. Suppose that you moved into a new home in an unfamiliar neighborhood. You didn't know that you are living in a crime-ridden neighborhood where your neighbors are criminals. There are three main entrances to your house: the front door, the back door, and the garage. You trust the people in your neighborhood because they smile at you and don't look harmful. So you go to work every day, leaving all the main entrances unlocked.

Would the ignorance of the criminal activities in your new neighborhood excuse you from being burgled? Surely, you would be looted! In fact, it won't take them long to clean you out if you do not secure your house. Definitely, you got into this problem because you have no knowledge of the crime activities in your neighborhood.

Just like a house with three main points of entry, so is our spiritual house—our body is the temple of God (1 Corinthians 6:19). It has its own front door (the eyes), the back door (the ears), and the garage (our thoughts). The eyes, the ears, and our thoughts are entry points for spirits to enter into us. The unfortunate thing is that many times we honestly don't even know we've thrown our spiritual "house" open or have it unlocked, or failed to have our security activated (by not fully living in Christ).

Such ignorance pleases the enemy and his companions because they desperately need to get into someone. One of the ways we give the devil free legal access into our lives is by indulging in sin. Sin is the gate-pass for the demonic spirits. The Bible provides us with the knowledge of the debilitating power of sin. The experience of Adam and Eve remains a reference point. Knowledge of how the enemy gets into us is as important as knowing how to fight him. You can't keep the doors of your life open to the devil and expect to effectively fight him.

The fact is that the enemy outwits us where we are ignorant. **2 Corinthians 2:11** says, *"And we do this so that we may not be outwitted by Satan; for we are not ignorant of his designs")*. If we do not have knowledge of an enemy fully armed to kill or destroy us, how can we survive the invasion of his armies? How can we win the spiritual battles confronting us daily if we have no knowledge of the superior weapons of warfare available for us to use to fight the war?

It is more saddening that many Christians have no knowledge on how to use the spiritual weapons given to them. Knowledge on how the enemy operates provides us with a good fighting strategy as well as effective intelligence. We must have knowledge of the strengths, weaknesses, type of armament, and probable warfare strategies of the enemy we are fighting against. This is important in spiritual warfare because the kingdom of darkness is tremendously armed!

You are stronger than your enemy by how much of him you know and less of you that he knows. You disadvantage your enemy by what you have in your knowledge bank about him. You are knowledge away from your victory!

How can you be skillful in the art of spiritual warfare without the proper knowledge of the enemy? It is like driving your car to an unknown destination without a guide. God has provided for us the Bible with which we shall know the whole armor to be worn in fighting against the enemy (Ephesians 6:10-17)—and it is our responsibility to study it in order to make incredible knowledge-guided spiritual engagements! Good knowledge of the Bible provides us with all the intelligence we need to know about how the enemy behaves or operates. Studying the Bible equips us with tactical survival skills to deal with the enemy.

Therefore, if we are going to encounter deceit, the best defensive ploy is to have knowledge. When a person knows the Truth, that person cannot be deceived. Consequently, when it comes to the armor of God, the first step in fighting against the wiles and deceitful methods of the devil is to know the Truth. *"Stand, therefore, and fasten the belt of Truth around your waist"* (Ephesians 6:14).

Make the Bible your companion!

Look, I tell you one thing: The enemy is afraid of you when he knows that you know (1) his strengths and weaknesses, (2) your authority in Christ, and (3) your weapons and how to use them. How would you know that you are the Lords battle ax if not by knowing who the Bible says that you are (Jeremiah 51:20)! It is the knowledge of the Bible that alerts you that there's a spiritual war going on—and that you are in that war. If you are not well informed about your enemy, you will get deformed by the enemy! Many have been deformed by the devil!

The devil can't ambush you if you know that you are at war and you are ever prepared. God says to you: BE PREPARED! BE PREPARED every time!! BE PREPARED everywhere!!! Soldiers are always prepared to fight. Similarly, the soldiers of Christ should always be in a state of readiness. So, BE PREPARED always!

LET US PRAY!

1. Reflect on how this reflection on *"Knowledge"* ministers to you.

2. Pray and ask God for the forgiveness of your sins using **Psalm 51.**

3. Put on the full armor of God using *"The Warrior's Prayer"* (see page 16).

4. Pray *"The Act of Spiritual Communion"* prayer (see page 17).

5. Pray **Psalm 139** (God's perfect knowledge of man).

6. Holy Spirit, grant me the grace to grow in the knowledge of Your great Love and Truth, in the name of Jesus Christ.

7. Pray for a genuine desire for the deeper knowledge of God. Lord Jesus, I desire (pray in the name of Jesus Christ):
   a. To know more of You;
   b. To have a heart and mind that is focused upon You;
   c. To have a deep desire to diligently study Your Word.

8. Armed with the knowledge of spiritual warfare (pray in the name of Jesus Christ):
   a. I run through enemy troops unharmed;
   b. I leap over walls of limitations;
   c. I breakthrough into new realms of unlimited possibilities and opportunities;
   d. I break forth into a realm which has no limits and no boundaries;
   e. I decree that my spheres of influence are now enlarged.

9. Thank the Lord Jesus Christ and cover this prayer with His Most Precious Blood (7 times).

DAY 17 - Part II: Warfare Prayers

Note:

- From the mouth of God comes Words that give understanding and knowledge **(Psalm 119:130)**. We ought to seek spiritual knowledge by meditating in the Bible (The Word of God).

- It is better to seek knowledge and understanding from the Lord than to gain silver and much fine gold **(Proverbs 16:16)**.

1. Sing songs to the Lord as the Holy Spirit leads.

2. Use **Psalm 51** to ask God for the forgiveness of your sins.

3. Put on the full armor of God using *"The Warrior's Prayer"* (see page 16).

4. Pray *"The Act of Spiritual Communion"* prayer (see page 17).

5. I declare that the knowledge of God shall reign in this generation until the second coming of our Lord Jesus Christ, in the name of Jesus Christ.

6. Holy Spirit, open my eyes and ears to spiritual knowledge, in the name of Jesus Christ.

7. I overthrow and overrule the assignments of spirits that will cause spiritual blindness, deafness, and my voice to be silenced, in the name of Jesus Christ.

8. I pierce darkness with the light of godly knowledge, in the name of Jesus Christ. Therefore, in the name of Jesus Christ:
   a. I gain God-inspired illumination, wisdom, insight, and power;
   b. Darkness shall not comprehend, apprehend, or prevent godly knowledge from fully manifesting in my life.

9. I have the knowledge that *"The Son of God was revealed ... to destroy the works of the devil"* **(1 John 3:8)**. Therefore, in the

name of Jesus Christ:
a. I lift up my voice like a trumpet in Zion to declare that Jesus Christ is Lord;
b. I declare that God rules and reigns over my life;
c. All the works of the devil against my life are destroyed.

10. Armed with the knowledge of spiritual warfare, I break through all anti-destiny, anti-purpose, anti-passion, anti-divine, anti-success, anti-prayer, anti-Christ demonic forces, in the name of Jesus Christ.

11. Armed with the knowledge of spiritual warfare *(pray in the name of Jesus Christ):*
a. I take authority over every spirit that projects accidents to my life;
b. By divine firewalls and smokescreens, I declare myself and everything associated with me invisible to the eyes of the enemies;
c. I command every satanic GPS system to begin to malfunction and irreparably destroyed.
d.
12. Armed with the knowledge of spiritual warfare, I possess my possessions by FORCE **(Matthew 11:12)**, in the name of Jesus Christ!

13. By divine knowledge, I live, I breathe, and I have my being in Jesus Christ **(Acts 17:28)**—in the name of Jesus Christ.

14. Begin to thank the Lord Jesus Christ for the conquest granted through this prayer:
a. Thank You, Lord Jesus Christ, for teaching me how spiritual knowledge can be used to fight a spiritual war;
b. Thank You, Lord Jesus Christ, for the wealth of knowledge You have given us in the Bible;
c. Offer songs of thanksgiving or pray Psalm 148.
15. I cover this prayer with the Most Precious Blood of Jesus Christ (7 times).

Chapter 9

Agreement Prayer

"After this, the Lord appointed seventy-two others and sent them two by two ahead of him to every town and place where he was about to go."

(Luke 10:1)

"For where two or three are gathered in my name, I am there among them"

(Matthew 18:20)

[Other suggested Bible passages to read:
I Samuel 14: 1-17, I Samuel 10:26, Acts 1: 14, Amos. 3:3,
I Corinthians 1:10-11, Psalm133:1].

DAY 18 - Part I: Reflection

Unity is strength, people say. Little can a broomstick do; but when many, the broom sweeps clean. A threefold cord is not easily broken, you know! Studies show that lions have more hunting success rate when hunting a prey as a group than when it is just a lone lion doing the hunting. Jesus appointed His disciples and *"sent them two by two"* (Luke 10:1, NKJV). No wonder **Ecclesiastes 4:9, 12** says, *"Two are better than one; because they have a good reward for their labor...And if one prevail against him, two shall withstand him."*

This is true because there is great power in working together with undivided purpose. Two or more people agreeing together in fervent prayer unleash tremendous spiritual power. Truly, there is more power in agreement prayer than in the prayer of a divided people. When we pray in agreement, the Lord Himself is there with us and in agreement with us. Believers are one with Christ. **Matthew 18:19-20** says, *"Again, truly I tell you, if two of you agree on earth about anything you ask, it will be done for you by my Father in heaven. For where two or three are gathered in my name, I am there among them."*

In spiritual warfare, there is no substitute for unity and no progress whatsoever without it. The military never sends people into battle by themselves. It is always two-by-two at a minimum. As soldiers of Christ, we must understand that Jesus intends for it to be the same way with us as we fight against the kingdom of darkness. God fights alone but He never intended us to fight alone.

What do you think saved the life of Peter when King Herod imprisoned him, waiting to execute him after the Passover? It was the agreement prayer of the Church, for *"While Peter was kept in prison, the Church prayed fervently to God for him"* (Acts 12:5). It was the fervent prayer of the Church that moved God to send an Angel to rescue Peter from prison. This was an answer and the result of their agreement prayer. Striving together in prayer brings deliverance! *"How good and pleasant it is when God's people live [and fellowship] together in unity!"* (Psalm 133:1). This was not the case when James was arrested, leading to him being beheaded by Herod (**Acts 12:2**). Agreement prayer is a mighty weapon against the move of the enemy.

Do we really comprehend the magnitude of this weapon that Heaven offered to us? Other than the Lord Himself, no power or principality in either the natural or the spiritual realms can match the power of His people when they are charging against the enemy in corporate prayer. In fact, the devil literally shakes in his boots when God's people are praying together in the atmosphere of harmony!

The enemy knows that agreement prayer is a powerful weapon that we have with us. He doesn't like it and that is why he schemes discord or division among the brethren. The weapon of fellowship destroys Satan's ability to divide and conquer.

The enemy cannot stand against the assaults of God's people praying with one accord under the Power and the anointing of the Holy Spirit. We learn that the mighty exploits on the Pentecost day itself took place as the disciples *"were all together in one place"* praying with one accord **(Acts 2:1)**.

Even the devil and his kingdom of darkness come together in agreement against the Saints of the Most High God. Did the Scripture not tell us that, *"They shall surely gather together"* **(Isaiah 54:15)**? Unity of evil murdered Stephen **(Acts 7:57)**. God saw the evil intent and unity of the builders of the tower of Babel **(Genesis 11:5-8)**. Jesus tells us that every kingdom that is divided against itself cannot stand **(Matthew 12:25)**.

Two-by-two is a warfare strategy. Every Christian needs a "wingman." Where is your "wingman"? Who is the Aaron raising your hands in prayer when you need help **(Exodus 17:12-14)**. Again, remember the power of agreement prayers as *"... one chase[s] a thousand, and two put ten thousand to flight..."* **(Deuteronomy 32:30)**. It cannot be overemphasized that agreement prayer disarms the enemy and sets us up for victory.

LET US PRAY!

1. Reflect on how this reflection on *"Agreement Prayer"* ministers to you.

2. Pray and ask God for the forgiveness of your sins using **Psalm 51**. Make the following prayers in the name of Jesus Christ:

a. Pardon our sins and heal our divisions that we may grow in love, unity, and holiness together as your children;

b. May all Christian people throughout the world attain the unity for which You prayed for in John 17;

c. Renew in us the Power of the Holy Spirit that we may be a sign of unity and a means of its growth.

3. Put on the full armor of God using *"The Warrior's Prayer"* (see page 16).

4. Pray *"The Act of Spiritual Communion"* prayer (see page 17).

5. Pray **Psalm 78:5-26** (pay attention to verse 5 that says, *"The Lord made an agreement with Jacob and gave the teachings to Israel, which He commanded our ancestors to teach to their children"* (NCV)).

6. I come into an agreement with the prayers of all believers all over the world. As a result of this unity prayer, Heavenly explosive fireworks are generated that wreck the kingdom of darkness—in the name of Jesus Christ.

7. I decree that as I make this prayer, I come into agreement with the Supreme Court of Heaven, in the name of Jesus Christ. Therefore, in the name of Jesus Christ:

a. I blind satanic networks, communication, and alliances;

b. Evil collaborators and collaborations are unveiled and exposed;

c. Let those who have gathered against me be scattered, never to be regrouped again;

d. Let their eyes be darkened that they see not again, and let their ears be blocked that they hear not again;

e. Let them seek their sustenance out of desolate places.

8. Thank the Lord Jesus Christ and cover this prayer with His Most Precious Blood (7 times).

DAY 19 - Part II: Warfare Prayers

Note:

- The Holy Spirit brings harmony (unity) when we are agreeing and coming together in prayer. Success in warfare is strongly dependent upon oneness in prayer.

- Agreement prayer defeats Satan. God greatly desires the unity of His people in prayer!

1. Sing songs to the Lord as the Holy Spirit leads.

2. Use **Psalm 51** to ask God for the forgiveness of your sins. Make the following prayers, in the name of Jesus Christ:
   a. I renounce all agreements that I have made with the devil;
   b. I reverse channels of satanic contaminations with the Most Precious Blood of Jesus Christ;
   c. Pray and ask the Lord Jesus Christ to purify your soul and spirit with His Most Precious Blood.

3. Put on the full armor of God using *"The Warrior's Prayer"* (see page 16).

4. Pray *"The Act of Spiritual Communion"* prayer (see page 17).

5. Come, Lord Jesus, and make us one, in the name of Jesus Christ!

6. *"When the king heard what the man of God cried out against the altar at Bethel, Jeroboam stretched out his hand from the altar, saying, "Seize him!" But the hand that he stretched out against him withered so that he could not draw it back to himself. The altar also was torn down, and the ashes poured out from the altar, according to the sign that the man of God had given by the word of the Lord"* (**1 Kings 13:4-5**). Therefore, in the name of Jesus Christ, I am in agreement with **1 Kings 13:4-5** that:
   a. Every evil hand stretched out against me must be paralyzed;

    b. Every evil altar raised against me must be torn down and burnt to ashes;

    c. Every evil arrow projected to harm me or my loved ones, or our belongings must backfire;

    d. Every "Jeroboam" fashioning evil against me must be covered with reproach and dishonor.

        i. A tempest of judgment is against "Jeroboam";

        ii. A storm of displeasure is against "Jeroboam";

        iii. From today, every "Jeroboam" in my life shall walk in fear;

        iv. The arrows of this prayer shall torment "Jeroboam" by day and by night.

7. Lord Jesus, I ask that all Christians be in full spiritual agreement with one another, in the name of Jesus Christ.

8. I am in agreement with 1 John 4:4 that *"Greater is He that is in me than he that is in the world"*! Therefore, in the name of Jesus Christ:

    a. The gates of Hell shall not prevail against me (nor the Church)!

    b. No weapon of the enemy formed against me (or the Church) shall prosper!

    c. Many shall receive healing and deliverance today through this prayer;

    d. I prohibit the devil access to anything that belong to me.

9. I am in agreement with **Psalm 69:22-28** that the enemy's table of gathering has become a snare before them, in the name of Jesus Christ.

    a. I overturn their table! I overturn them!!

    b. That which had been for their welfare, let it become a trap;

    c. Let their habitation be desolate;
       I resist advancements to destroy my life and family;

    d. I break out of satanic bondage and resist bewitchment.

10. I break free from all evil thoughts, projections, suggestions, and innuendos that have been designed to discourage, mislead, or confuse me in life—in the name of Jesus Christ.

11. Begin to thank the Lord Jesus Christ for the conquest granted through this prayer:
    a. Thank You, Lord Jesus Christ, for teaching me how agreement prayer can be used to fight a spiritual war;
    b. Offer songs of thanksgiving or pray **Psalm 147**.

12. I cover this prayer with the Most Precious Blood of Jesus Christ (7 times).

Chapter 10

Faith

"For whatever is born of God overcomes the world: and this is the victory that overcomes the world, even our faith."

(1 John 5:4)

"Through faith [they] subdued kingdoms, worked righteousness, obtained promises, stopped the mouths of lions, quenched the violence of fire, escaped the edge of the sword, out of weakness were made strong, waxed valiant in fight, turned to flight foreign armies."
(Hebrews 11:33-34)

[Other suggested Bible passages to read:
Hebrews 11:1-40, Ephesians 6:16, Daniel 3:16-28,
Daniel 6:1–28, Esther 5-10].

DAY 20 - Part I: Reflection

The devil is not afraid of a baby Christian. However, if that baby Christian is allowed to grow and mature in the Christian faith—if he is allowed to learn about spiritual warfare, about his weapons, and how to work in tandem with the Holy Spirit— then he becomes a real threat to the kingdom of darkness. That is why the enemy puts so much energy in stunting our Christian growth so as to prevent us from engaging our faith in utilizing our spiritual weapons.

When our faith in God begins to grow, the devil takes notice and begins to get worried. Then he begins to fight us. We become a serious threat to him when our faith makes us a moving fire. At this point, he cannot easily have his way with his many attacks. A baby Christian, therefore, has to grow in faith as to become a threat to the evil forces of the kingdom of darkness. Faith is critical in our Christian journey.

We may have all the warrior's weapons at our disposal but without faith, we are simply helpless. How can an Air Force officer fly his high-tech jet fighter if he is afraid of heights? He must first, have faith that he will not fall from the great heights during combat operations. Just as a runner must run more to be a better runner, so he overcomes the fear of the great heights by, first of all, practicing low-level flying until he graduates into greater altitudes.

Faith, like muscles, grows only when exercised. We grow our faith with Prayer, the Word, and Action. In fact, Faith is Praying and taking Action on God's Word. The enemy hates it when we Pray and take Action on God's Word because he knows that he will be defeated. He knows the power of faith and what it can do!

Faith is the key to unlocking the power of God that is within us.

Faith is a tremendous weapon of warfare that we have. It is a defensive and offensive weapon! As the shield of faith deflects the fiery darts, so the word of faith dislodges the mountains and sends into disarray the enemy's army. Much can be accomplished with many prayers but, pertaining to faith, much can be accomplished with a little faith. Jesus says, *"Truly I tell you, if you have faith as small as a mustard seed, you can say to this mountain, 'Move from here to there,' and it will move. Nothing will be impossible for you"* (Matthew 17:20). Prayer may be mightier than a bullet but faith is mightier than an army!

We don't really understand how much power our faith in God carries until we engage the lever of faith. In this book, the importance of prayer in the operations of spiritual warfare has been emphatically stressed. However, prayer without faith is not different from a bird perching on an anthill and saying to the ground, *"I am standing far above you."* The bird needs to realize that even the anthill upon which it stands is the same ground from where it flew. It has not made any progress at all!

Faith is the opposite of fear. That means that we are to resist fear and unbelief by being steadfast or firm in our faith. The enemy uses fear to attack our faith. Our faith in God breaks off the chains of fear and doubt in our lives. Hebrews Chapter 11 wrote a lot about faith. Let's pay attention to the following verses:

> *"[These were men] through faith subdued kingdoms, worked righteousness, obtained promises, stopped the mouths of lions, quenched the violence of fire, escaped the edge of the sword, out of weakness were made strong, waxed valiant in fight, turned to flight foreign armies"*
> **(Hebrews 11:33-34).**

In this Scripture, we see how the children of God in times past were able to defeat their enemies with their faith. Take note of all the great exploits they were able to accomplish with their faith:

1. They subdued kingdoms
2. They worked righteousness
3. They obtained God's promises
4. They shut the mouths of lions
5. They quenched the violence of fire
6. They escaped death
7. Out of weakness, they were made strong

8. They waxed valiant in battle
9. They defeated the enemy armies

This is still true for us believers today *"for whatever is born of God conquers the world. And this is the victory that conquers the world, our faith"* (1 John 5:4). It is by our faith that we overcome the enemy. It is by our faith that the impossible is made possible, limitations challenged, mountains dislodged, strongholds destroyed, and God's promises received (e.g., healings and miracles).

LET US PRAY!
1. Reflect on how this reflection on *"Faith"* ministers to you.

2. Pray and ask God for the forgiveness of your sins using **Psalm 51.**

3. Put on the full armor of God using *"The Warrior's Prayer"* (see page 16).

4. Pray *"The Act of Spiritual Communion"* prayer (see page 17).

5. Pray **Psalm 62** (a prayer for trust in God alone).

6. Lord Jesus, may I have *"a place among those who are sanctified by faith in [You]"* (**Acts 26:18**), in the name of Jesus Christ.

7. Lord Jesus, in times of trouble, may I never doubt Your saving help and Your watchful Presence in my life, in the name of Jesus Christ.

8. Lord Jesus, *"I believe; help my unbelief!"* (**Mark 9:24**). In the name of Jesus Christ:
   a. Show me what I must do to follow You unwaveringly;
   b. Make Your path clear to me and give me the strength to follow it.

9. With faith in the Lord Jesus Christ, I have authority over all

destiny altering activities, satanic sanctions and impositions, in the name of Jesus Christ.

10. **Faith in Action:** What's the number one challenge you are facing right now?
    a. Today, visualize placing it on an Altar of Jesus Christ;
    b. Then lift up your hands in worship and praise to God (begin worshipping and praising God);
    c. Note: Even if your situation doesn't change as expected, your heart will. Give God glory and say, *"Lord Jesus, I offer this situation to You: 'Your will be done'"* (Matthew 6:10).

11. Thank the Lord Jesus Christ and cover this prayer with His Most Precious Blood (7 times).

DAY 21 - Part II: Warfare Prayers

Note:
- Let us tap into the Power of Christ through the warrior's faith, love, and prayer.

- Faith says to us: Don't wait to understand everything to believe; rather, believe and you will begin to understand.

- Please, know that:
    1. Our Faith is the object of Satan's attack **(Jude 3)**;
    2. Our Faith is constantly being tried **(I Peter 1: 7)**;
    3. Our Faith must be pursued **(I Timothy 6: 11)**;
    4. Our Faith must be fought for **(I Timothy 6: 12)**;
    5. Our Faith must be defended **(Jude 3)**.

1. Sing songs to the Lord as the Holy Spirit leads.

2. Use **Psalm 51** to ask God for the forgiveness of your sins.
    a. If I have inadvertently hurt or disappointed anyone, ask for mercy and forgiveness;
    b. Lord Jesus Christ, free me from the stronghold of offense,

un-forgiveness, bitterness, hatred, and indifference;
   c.   I repent of my sins. Thank You, Lord Jesus Christ, for forgiving me.

3.   Put on the full armor of God using *"The Warrior's Prayer"* (see page 16).

4.   Pray *"The Act of Spiritual Communion prayer"* (see page 17).

5.   Lord Jesus, grant me the light of faith, in the name of Jesus Christ.

6.   Lord Jesus, may I express my faith in You no matter what it costs or how foolish I look, in the name of Jesus Christ.

7.   Lord Jesus, I want my faith to grow: Please, help me to see my faith grow, in the name of Jesus Christ.

8.   Lord Jesus, walk with me through every burning furnace experience I pass through, in the name of Jesus Christ:
   a.   Grant me faith and courage of Shadrach, Meshach, and Abednego that I may never renounce your name in the face of trials;
   b.   Help me put my faith into action.

9.   Lord Jesus, fortify my faith with courage and give me enduring hope that I may never waver in my trust in You, in the name of Jesus Christ.

10. With the eyes of faith in the Lord Jesus Christ through this prayer:
   a.   I see mountains melting;
   b.   I plow my way through demonic barricades;
   c.   I see divine intervention and miracles coming;
   d.   I see every situation and circumstance come into divine alignment;
   e.   I see every curse reversed.

11. With faith, I excavate seeds planted by the enemy in my mind, my soul, and my spirit, in the name of Jesus Christ. I decree, in the name of Jesus Christ, that:
    a. They shall not take root;
    b. They shall not be incubated, nurtured, nourished, fed or watered;
    c. They are destroyed now!

12. With faith, I receive only that which emanates from the mind of God. I decree, in the name of Jesus Christ, that:
    a. Seeds of hope, seeds of faith, prayerfulness, destiny, power, success, and righteousness are planted in me;
    b. I shall not miscarry my seeds. I carry them full term!

13. With faith in the Lord Jesus Christ, I decree that every demonic prison is opened, in the name of Jesus Christ.
    a. I release ......(*pick from the following list)* from prison, in the name of Jesus Christ.

       - My future
       - My anointing
       - My family
       - My ministry
       - My nation
       - The Government

    b. I release.....(*use the above list in prayer point #13a*) from being controlled by demonic forces, in the name of Jesus Christ;
    c. I demand that every "Pharaoh" must let .....(*use the above list in prayer point #13a*) go, in the name of Jesus Christ;
    d. I break out of confinement and all forms of bondage;
    e. I decree that whom the Son sets free is free indeed **(John 8:36)**. Therefore, in the name of Jesus Christ:
       i. I will not allow my past to negatively affect my future;
       ii. I break free from soul ties and entanglements that undermine who I am in Christ;
       iii. Every debt in my life is paid for by the Most Precious Blood of Jesus Christ;

    iv. I am freed from all those who have sold me out in life;

    v. I decree that today is the dawning of a new day;

    vi. I am fully liberated today: In the name of Jesus Christ!!!

14. **Hebrews 11:33-34** says that *"Through faith [they] subdued kingdoms, worked righteousness, obtained promises, stopped the mouths of lions, quenched the violence of fire, escaped the edge of the sword, out of weakness were made strong, waxed valiant in fight, turned to flight foreign armies."* Ask God to give you the kind of faith:

    a. That subdues kingdoms, works righteousness, leads to obtaining promises, closes the mouths of the enemy, quenches the violence of fire, and cheats untimely death;

    b. That makes one strong in the place of weakness, makes one wax valiant in fight, and that turns to flight the enemy armies.

15. **Intercessory Prayer:** Ask God to raise a generation of stewards whose faith can move mountains, challenge limitations, counterfeit strongholds, and destroy wicked schemes of the enemy—pray in the name of Jesus Christ.

16. **Faith in Action:** With your faith, begin to speak to the mountains in your life **(Matthew 17:20)**. Make the following prayers in the name of Jesus Christ:

    a. Peter spoke to the "mountain" of lameness **(Acts 3:1-6)**. Speak to every "mountain" of lameness in your life to move to the abyss;

    b. Peter spoke to the "mountain" of palsy in Aeneas **(Acts 9:32-34)**. Speak to every "mountain" of sickness in your life to move to the abyss;

    c. Peter spoke to the "mountain" of death in Dorcas **(Acts 9:40)**. Speak to every "mountain" of death in your life to move to the abyss.

17. Begin to thank the Lord Jesus Christ for the conquest granted through this prayer:
    a. Lord Jesus, I thank You for the gift of faith;
    b. Thank You, Lord Jesus Christ, for teaching me how my faith in You can be used to fight a spiritual war;
    c. Offer songs of thanksgiving or pray **Psalm 146.**

18. I cover this prayer with the Most Precious Blood of Jesus Christ (7 times).

Epilogue

Think. Think. I say, think! Think of one thing that God is telling you after reading this book. Could HE be asking you, "Where are your armor and Weapons?" Suppose God asked this question to a tortoise, it would rightly respond, "I carry my armor-shell wherever I go. The ants or bees would say, "We carry our stinging weapons everywhere. The scorpion would respond, "I carry the poison you gave me to protect myself." So would the lions, porcupines, snakes, spiders, bulls, and so on. They all carry their weapons all the time: whether eating, playing, sleeping, or hunting. They don't drop their Weapons. They understand that their survival is tied to using their weapons and knowing how to use them.

Regrettably, as for many people of God—people who God created in His own image—they have dropped their armor and weapons meant to protect them from being casualties in the hands of the devil and his kingdom of darkness. Let us go to the ants or the scorpions and learn how to be battle-ready, always carrying our weapons!

In answering this question, I hope you are not among the countless Christians who have dropped their spiritual weapons and armor. I pray this book motivates you to be like the bees: always armed and dangerous! Always ready to fight!

The difference between a victor and a victim lies in whether you carry your armor and weapons with you all the time (not just some time) or not. *The Warrior's Weapons* has expounded the spiritual weapons. Use your weapons! Use them always! Use this book! Get it for your children and friends.

God bless you!

War Against Python and Snake Spirits

The first Biblical prophecy in Genesis 3:15 simply reveals a salient truth: There is a spiritual hostility and conflict between the righteous and the devil, the ancient serpent. God wants us to engage the ancient serpent in a battle. He wants us to use the authority He has given to us to smash the serpent's head. Unfortunately, so many people of God are bound by demonic forces but do not know how to be free. The proliferation of python and snake spirits in this end time has resulted in an epidemic of people living in spiritual bondage. These python and snake spirits have aggressive appetite for destinies to swallow! War Against Python And Snake Spirits is an attempt to address this problem.

The Warrior's Weapons (Volume 1 & 2)

Never in the history of mankind has there been an era of war like ours. We could smell war in the air. While the media reminds us of physical wars, the struggles we go through everyday remind us of spiritual wars. In a sense, it seems that there is an outbreak of demonic hostilities. Now that we know that we are at war, so what? What are we going to do about it? If we are to survive these trying times in which we live, it is imperative that we learn how to effectively use the weapons of warfare against the devil and his companions. In this book, you have everything you need to become armed and dangerous against every adversary that threatens you and your destiny. The book presents some strategic weapons from our spiritual arsenal and how they are to be used against the kingdom of darkness.

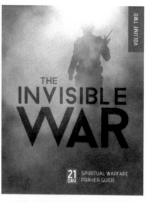

The Invisible War (Volume 1 & 2)

Spiritual war is a fierce battle that is not visible to the ordinary eyes. The war is invisible, but the impact is real. All of us are in the midst of this war which rages underneath the earth, inside the waters, in the air, and in the heavenlies. The battle goes on irrespective of whether we know it or not, or whether we believe it or not. There is no break in the war, no causal leave, and no cease-fire! This occurs every single day both during the day and night. The Invisible War is a fire-loaded warfare book prayerfully packaged to make you dangerous against every spiritual adversary that threatens your destiny. It is written to be engaging as you find in it a blend of real-life experiences, history, Scriptures, storytelling, and prayers.